'An incredible story of the transfo[...] to shape and direct our lives, emp[...] hurdle that stands in the way [...] callings. Amelia's faithful obe[...] encouragement to us all.'
Rev Manoj Raithatha, Minister of Pinner Baptist Church and Chair of the Board of the UK Evangelical Alliance

'Journeying with Amelia, through the twists and turns of her life, I was captivated by her story. Coming to the UK from Pakistan, an arranged marriage, then becoming a priest... What an amazing lady, and what an incredible God! Inspirational, encouraging, exciting and informative.'
Sheila Jacobs, editor, award-winning writer, author of A Little Book of Rest

'*The Priest from Pakistan* is an inspirational testimonial story containing dreams and visions, kindness and grief, courageously and devotedly shared and expressing explicitly the holy intervention and presence of God in Amelia's life. The awesomeness of the Holy One is shared in the simple manner it is experienced by the author.

'I recommend this experiential book. It is a reminder of life's wonder and frailty, yet God's faithfulness and finality.'
Alwin J Samuel, Bishop of Sialkot, Pakistan

'I commend this book to anyone who wants to know what it is to walk with God and follow His voice. Amelia has written an honest and inspirational book of faith and God's faithfulness. At times I felt deeply moved, and by the end of the book I felt as though I too had been on a journey that has been courageous, loving and full of trust in God the Father, Son and Holy Spirit.'
Rev Julia Jagannath, Rector of St Mary with St Richard, Northolt

'This is a story of an ordinary person who, in response to Jesus, offers herself for His purposes, wherever it will lead. Amelia's journey, in so many ways against the odds, demonstrates that the same Jesus who called Peter from being a fisherman to a leader in his Church can call anyone today into leadership if they are open to Him. Amelia writes with endearing humility, and as a result points to Jesus as the one who can do more than we ask or imagine.'

Rev Christopher Ramsay, Vicar of St George's Southall and Willesden Director of Mission

'Two different continents, two different shapes of church life: Amelia's story binds the two together. By reading her personal story of how just one seed has germinated and grown, we are privileged to glimpse something of the ordinary ways in which the Word of God flourishes in very different cultures. Amelia's warm-hearted story is very personal and yet enlarges our vision to glimpse more of the "manifold wisdom of God" (Ephesians 3:10).'

Rev John Root, former Vicar of St James' Alperton

'This is an inspiring story of the first Pakistani woman to be ordained a priest in the Diocese of London. Amelia came to the UK to be with her husband and discovered she was being called to ministry. This book tells the story of her courageous and faithful journey, despite her lack of English, despite having no role models or mentors, despite coming from another country and culture, to her ordination to the priesthood and her work beyond. This is a fascinating story of a woman determined to respond to the call of God, against all the odds.'

Rev Alison Christian, retired parish priest and advocate for spiritual direction

'This is an honest and uplifting account of Amelia's journey of faith.'

Linda Sweeting, teacher

'Amelia's book gives a fascinating insight into both the challenges of a family coming to faith in Christ from a different religious background and the cultural differences between East and West. As she and Stanley negotiated the challenges of life in the UK and Christian ministry together, it is clear to see the guidance of the Lord Jesus in their lives. Amelia's ministry has touched many lives, and she is much loved and appreciated by people not only of Pakistani origin but also British, Indian and Sri Lankan.'
Geoff Lumley, former teacher and lay chaplain

'Having read *The Priest from Pakistan*, I could feel and see the Lord working in the life of Amelia. She is a very humble and dedicated servant of God with a hope to continue serving the Lord and His people. Each chapter of the book brings forth a lesson for readers, encouraging them to be strong in faith, to trust in the Lord and to receive blessings with the spirit of acknowledgement. My heartfelt prayer for Amelia is that God uses her more and more for His glory.'
Professor Dr Sarah Safdar, former Dean of Social Sciences, University of Peshawar, Pakistan; Member of the National Commission for Minorities, Government of Pakistan; Member of the National Commission on the status of woman, Government of Pakistan

'Sister Amelia's journey to ordination as Pakistan's first woman priest is inspiring on cultural, theological and spiritual levels. This easy-to-read account is a crystallisation of a very difficult-to-live life. This faith-strengthening narration of a real Christian daughter's experiences will find a place among Christian classics.'
Dr Akhtar Injeeli, CEO Injeeli Consultancy Ltd

'It is very interesting to read of Amelia's journey, and the varied cross-cultural experiences she has encountered. What strikes me

most is her humble lifelong desire to get to know her Lord better, and to follow wherever He leads.'
David Shaw, chair of St James' Alperton World Church Committee

'Amelia has written a fascinating account of her life's journey from childhood in Pakistan to ordained ministry in the Church of England at a time when the CofE was grappling with an increasingly multicultural constituency and strong divisions over women's ministry. By her own admission, Amelia is quiet and takes time to process things, and has learned over the years to distinguish her own thoughts from God's "small, sweet voice" speaking through different channels. Her journey has not been easy, but there is no bitterness, only a steady trust in God's loving purposes. She touches on so many matters, including how to adapt Pakistani family culture to a British context, and how to share Christ with migrants to the UK from the Indian subcontinent, aware that a strategy for one generation will not necessarily work for the next. On these pages, Amelia shares her love for Christ and what has helped her to nourish that relationship. Regrettably she does not share the recipe for her famous "Amelia's rice"!'
Rev Clive Main, Curate at St James Alperton 1996–2000

'Pakistan, being an Islamic state, is predominantly a male culture. In the 1950s, women leadership was beyond comprehension. Generally, girls were not encouraged in regard to education, any vocation or employment.

'"Can anything good come from Nazareth?" The writer comes from a remote area of Pakistan and was ordained as a priest in the Church of England. Though facing cultural shocks and other obstacles in the UK, she still believed that her "dream will come true".

'I am so thrilled to read her personal story. Focusing on "God's grace at work" is the hallmark of the writer. God has

promised that "my grace is sufficient" for you. For these reasons, I fully endorse this book.'
The Rev Prebendary Wilson E Gill, Dean of Cultural Diversity, Willesden Area, Diocese of London

'It has been a privilege to work with Rev Amelia and a joy to read her story. Amelia is just as you find her in her book: humble and self-effacing while filled with nugget after nugget of wisdom and courage. The story of where her passion to follow Jesus, perseverance in faith and heart to serve others has grown from is truly remarkable. Her book is gentle, and yet so important in chronicling her struggles and passion as she lives a life following Jesus as an outsider and a as a leader. Her vision of Jesus changed her life and led to her making a difference to the lives of so many others. I pray that you will learn from Amelia's experience and be as blessed by her as we have been.'
Rev Ali Taylor and Rev Steve Taylor, Vicars, St James' Alperton

'This book is a window into Amelia's life, a woman born and brought up in a Christian family in the Islamic Republic of Pakistan. It tells the story of how this girl goes on to become a priest in the United Kingdom, and how the foundation of biblical principles laid by her converted grandfather C L Jacob played a role in building a life with bricks of trust in the Lord.

'With each chapter and every word shining with grace, this book will help readers not only to grow spiritually but also to apply God's word to their lives.'
Akhtar Pervaiz, Deputy General Manager (Ret), Pakistan Steel Mills

'It has been an honour and pleasure to work with Rev Amelia for many years. Her presence was impactful in the shaping of St James' Church, Alperton. Her meekness in spirit and her faith in God were her strength, which helped her work through all the challenges put before her. This book portrays exactly that, alongside her commitment and faithfulness to God's calling.

Her story will help readers to overcome their own limitations and will encourage and inspire those working outside their comfort zones.'

Rev Ajay More, Associate Vicar, St John's Church, Greenhill, Harrow

The Priest from Pakistan
A Journey of Grace

Amelia Jacob

instant
apostle

First published in Great Britain in 2023

Instant Apostle
104 The Drive
Rickmansworth
Herts
WD3 4DU

The views and opinions expressed in this work are those of the author and do not necessarily reflect the views and opinions of the publisher.

British Library Cataloguing-in-Publication Data

A catalogue record for this book is available from the British Library.

This book and all other Instant Apostle books are available from Instant Apostle:

Website: www.instantapostle.com

Email: info@instantapostle.com

ISBN 978-1-912726-63-9

Printed in Great Britain.

Dedication

I would like to dedicate the book to my husband, Stanley Jacob. The whole story would not have come into existence or been accomplished without his support and encouragement.

And to God, who loves me unconditionally, who tried to seek my attention with a small, sweet voice through dreams and eventually met me at my lowest point, after I repented, and led me onto the right path. All praise and glory to His holy name, in Jesus Christ.

Contents

Introduction

Many years ago, I wrote my grandfather's story of how he accepted Christ Jesus as his Lord and Saviour. Later this thought developed into including my own story of meeting the risen Christ, one that eventually led me into church ministry. I dictated the first draft of this book back in 2011, but it then lay incomplete in my drawer for many years. When I retired, the time seemed right to take up the challenge again!

I was a non-stipendiary part-time priest. I took retirement in the beginning of 2020 and I could carry on ministering with a licence for three years, with 'permission to officiate'. I also worked as an after-school club coordinator for five afternoons a week and took retirement from that job in 2018.

I hope that this book will reach many for God, and help those who need clarification in their faith. I am sharing my journey from the very beginning, up until my recent official retirement from formal ministry. This book contains my personal experience of walking with Jesus after He found me and guided me through every step of my life. My firm belief is that because of the once-for-all sacrifice of Jesus on the cross, I am forgiven. He rose from

the dead and is among us through His Holy Spirit. I hope
that my story will benefit many in their journey of faith.
Amelia Jacob

Author's note

In this book I have talked about seeds and planting – as
you will see from the chapter titles.

The Christian faith has been described as beginning
with a 'seed', and the symbolism was used many times in
the parables of Jesus. Over time, my interest has grown in
'sowing'; the reality of seed becoming more real during
my Christian life. I have experienced the reality of faith
growing from a tiny seed and maturing like a well-
watered plant. You will see this reflected in the book!

1

Germinating Process

I believe the journey of our faith begins as soon as we come to a realisation of our existence in the world, even without a clear knowledge of our exact beliefs. We are trained to join in with our family's religious practices and rituals, if they have them, whether we agree with them or not. As we know, most faiths have traditions and practices to perform when a child is born into a family. Whether that child just blindly follows the faith they are born into or whether they have a mind to question and explore for themselves their reasons for believing and exploring the meaning of life, existence, and if there is a God, is another story. Faith can begin as small as a 'mustard seed' (Luke 13:19) and can grow as big as a tree.

In a conversation between Jesus and His disciples, He asked who the crowds thought He was. After hearing the various views, He asked Peter, as an *individual*, 'Who do you say I am?' and Peter replied, 'You are the Messiah, the Son of the living God' (Matthew 16:13-16).

My earliest memory goes back to the age of three, if not before, living with my siblings in Haripur Hazara, Pakistan, a small town in the north-western province,

Khyber Pakhtunkhwa. We lived in accommodation owned by the company where our father worked as a stenographer. I don't think there was any church nearby. We might well have been the only Christian family in the area. We were taught to pray before eating and to give thanks for all we had. I do have faint memories of a worship place in a nearby town and being there with the family over Christmas. They had a Christmas tree with flickering candles on it. It seems funny, but I wondered for many years after about how the candles were just burning and not setting the tree alight! When I grew up, I searched around to see if such candles really existed, not realising that they were actually electric!

Somehow, I knew that I was part of a Christian family living in a Muslim-majority country. I have strong memories of playing with my siblings and cousins when visiting my maternal grandparents' house in Manipur, a town near Faisalabad, where my mother's father was serving in his local church as a type of churchwarden. From what I remember, his duties included going on pastoral visits to church families to pray and offer support. He carried with him the electoral roll register for anyone who wished to pay their monthly contributions towards the church. Here we were surrounded by aunties and uncles (our mother's siblings) who loved and cared for us dearly.

I was born on 13th May 1952, in the town of Lyallpur,[1] Punjab, Pakistan, at St Raphael's Hospital, situated close

---

[1] On 1st September 1977 the name of the town was changed to Faisalabad in honour of King Faisal of Saudi Arabia who made several financial contributions to Pakistan.

to 'Dada's' vicarage – my father's father. Faisalabad is an average city; it could be called the Manchester of Pakistan because of the many textile industries present there.

Faisalabad is famous for its clock tower. Following a decision by Sir James Lyall, the Deputy Commissioner, the fFoundation was laid on 14th November 1905 by the British Lieutenant governor of Punjab Sir Charles Riwaz. The tower iss located in the older part of the city and in the centre of eight markets (bazaar). From a bird's eye view it looks like the Union Flag of the United Kingdom. This layout still exists today, and the locals refer to it as 'Ghanta Ghar' in Urdu, which means 'Hour House'. During festivals, the Mayor of Faisalabad delivers a speech at this site and hangs the flag at full mast.

I came to know that on the very day of my birth, my eldest aunty wrapped me up in a blanket and slipped me out of the hospital. She took me home to show to everyone, when I was still supposed to be under hospital care with my mother. Then she took me back to the hospital without the officials noticing anything! Being the first grandchild, I can only imagine the excitement that there must have been to see a glimpse of me sooner rather than later.

My Dada Chunilal lived in the city of Quetta, India (now part of Pakistan), with his siblings, before the partition of 1947 when India was divided and Pakistan came into existence. His family were Hindus by faith, Kshatriyas by caste (second in hierarchy in the Hindu caste system) and goldsmiths by profession. They were financially well off and socially well respected. When Dada was a high school student, on his way home he received Christian tracts from British missionaries. He read them all and something about the Christian faith touched his heart; especially, it was the words of the Lord's Prayer. He was convicted of the truth of God when calling God his 'Father'. On meeting the missionaries again, he enquired further and was given a Bible to read for himself. It was a new experience for him. Reading the Bible opened his eyes to the reality and existence of God, which he had never known – or maybe deep down he had always been searching for this truth.

He went to meet the local priest, who was also a Hindu convert. The priest advised him to be baptised into the Christian faith, which he was, a few years later at the age of twenty-five. This news, however, was not taken well by his family, especially by his mother, who was devastated; she was sad because of what she saw as his betrayal of the ancestral faith, but was also fearful that she would be losing him forever.

Converting to Christianity was like becoming one of the lowest of castes and betraying one's gods. Dada's family tried to convince him to convert back to Hinduism, but he stood firm. An initial consequence of now being seen as from a lower caste was that he was not allowed to come in the kitchen area for food; instead, his mother passed the food to him to take away to a separate area, where he ate alone.

Later, he was told to leave home and was given just a sheet to sleep on and a bowl to drink from. He left home forever and never looked back. He chose the new Christian name of Jacob as his surname and kept the initials of his first name, and so was known as C L Jacob.

Names are an important part of our identity, given by our parents. Some parents will choose according to the meaning of the name, and some just like the sound of the name. Some people might choose to change their name to a choice of their own, once they are older. It is interesting to note that God, when He calls people for His purposes and plans, often gives them a new name – such as Abram and Sarai (Abraham and Sarah), for example.

Dada sensed his calling to full-time ministry and was trained in Gujranwala Seminary, Pakistan's oldest Presbyterian seminary. Later he got married to an orphan girl, Jasmine, who had been raised by missionaries after both her parents died in a plague. After marriage, Dada and his new wife were placed in the town of Sheikhupura in Punjab, which had no established church. He started a house church fellowship there, until the first church building was constructed in 1925, where the congregation grew. He served in Sheikhupura for seven years, where four of his children were born. The fourth child, sadly, died in infancy. They lived in rented accommodation while a permanent vicarage was being built. After this, he was placed in the United Presbyterian Church in Lyallpur in 1933 and served there for twenty-eight years until his retirement, witnessing the Partition of India in 1947. There, four more of his children were born. Altogether, he and his wife had seven surviving children, four girls and three boys.

Dada's elder brother once visited him in Lyallpur, after Partition, to offer him his share of the family inheritance, but he refused to accept it, saying, 'I have left your religion and so I don't want to receive anything of yours.' His brother refused to drink or eat anything from Dada's house and never visited again. Much later on, during his retirement, at our family evening prayers, Dada often testified and quoted the words of Jesus from Luke 18:29-30:

> I assure you that everyone who has given up house or wife or brothers or parents or children, for the sake of the Kingdom of God, will be repaid many times over in this life, and will have eternal life in the world to come.
> (NLT)

Dada could not ever visit India to see his family after Partition, because of the government's restrictions on travel. It must have been heart-breaking for him, being rejected by his own mother and family and never seeing them again. Reminiscing, he once shared that he remembered fondly how his sister used to make his favourite dessert, using lots of different nuts. However, he did not seem to have any regrets in choosing to follow Jesus.

I took Dada as my role model. The thought of writing about his life initially came from a relative of mine about thirty years ago. This relative shared with my sister that our grandfather's life and ministry was so impressive that a book should be written about it. This idea stayed with me and I began to make links between Dada's life and my own. The more I thought about it, the more these thoughts began to expand into a fuller picture in my mind. I kept pondering on it and began to gather information from his children about his life and ministry. I noted that my own life story had its origins in his ministry.

Looking back at Dada's life, I am inspired to adopt the same kind of committed church ministry that he exercised.

While growing up, I remember seeing him in his study, reading and preparing sermons. The sermons were handwritten in a notebook. Sometimes he would sit in his rocking chair in the vicarage garden going over the sermons in his mind.

Also, I observed his regular prayer habit. First thing in the morning, in his study, on his knees beside his chair, he would spend time in prayer. I remember thinking this was an amazing way to begin the day! He always prayed prayers of thanksgiving and supplication out loud.

I treasure a paperweight in my study, which used to sit on his desk. It takes me back to my childhood. Dada would make regular visits to the surrounding areas on his pushbike to conduct evening prayer meetings. This he did wholeheartedly and with great dedication each week.

I must have been about five when I accompanied Dada to an evening worship meeting that was held in my primary school hall. It was late and I dozed off on the bench. I started crying with embarrassment but was picked up and sat next to Dada. On another occasion, I accompanied Dada to visit a very sick man. He prayed for him and I came to know later that the man died soon afterwards. Now I value the purpose of this ministry, when I serve in this capacity. Maybe accompanying Dada was a small vision of my future calling.

After many years in ministry, I still long to adopt the regular habit of kneeling down in silence, to pray and spend quality time with God. I hope that one day I will get into this sacred habit! I have always been encouraged by my spiritual director to begin my quiet time with five minutes and then increase gradually, so I am getting into the habit and valuing the spiritual enrichment. For me, prayer, thanksgiving and confession are a way of life and I take heart in it.

Holding evening family prayers is another habit that I always long to adhere to on a more regular basis, but it has its stops and starts all the time. Our family and community celebrations always begin with Scripture reading and prayers of blessings.

Dada's strong and clear faith and determination to follow Jesus have always inspired me, and the way he sacrificed all that he could have inherited for the sake of the gospel. As an act of remembrance, I bought a chair in St James Church, Alperton – where I ministered – with an inscribed plaque saying, 'Chunilal Jacob, a pioneer of our Christian heritage'. This opportunity was given when, in the new building of St James', the pews were replaced by the chairs. We could buy a chair and a plaque with an inscription of our choice, and that's what I did. It came as a pleasant surprise to know that I share my date of birth with Dada – and he was baptised on the same date as I got married.

I also learned from what did not work so well in my family and I have tried to avoid those things. I came to know that Dada was quite disciplined and strict with regard to his children's education and spiritual growth. All of them had to get up at 5am to read the Bible before breakfast or getting ready for school. This I understand was not received well by his children, though they all kept to the Christian faith and have been practising Christians throughout their lives. For my children, I held to the example given in the parable of the prodigal son in Luke 15, who learned from his mistakes when given the space and opportunity. I tried to give them the teaching and the example that I could, and left the rest to themselves and God.

Marriage was another important life matter on which I needed to have an opinion. Dada arranged our uncles and aunts' marriages, with careful attention being paid to matching them up with Christian families. All their marriages seemed to work. Marriage was for life. Once married, one had to live in obedience to make it work for the honour of God. Divorce was unacceptable within the local culture. Women had no other option, choice or support system to turn to.

I observed the ins and outs and saw some safety and protection within this system of marriage, and so decided to follow this family tradition for myself. In addition to this, I knew that in general I was not great at making the best choices! It was nearly half a century ago when I 'tied the knot' with my husband, Stanley, and I am not saying that the road has always been easy.

Of course, the world's view of marriage has dramatically changed over the years. With my children, I decided to give them a free choice within limits, believing that it is good to meet and get to know your prospective partner before committing to marriage. Marriage seems to be a complex issue now, and to make it last requires a lot of work! I believe in the rule of God – taking marriage as a covenant and remembering the commandment of love. The vows taken need to be valid for the rest of one's life. It might well be worth repeating such vows each wedding anniversary! The choice of a partner should be made with God's wisdom and clear guidance.

I am aware that some people reading this may have gone through a difficult and hard process of divorce, but

God is our loving Father who is capable of redeeming any situation and can use any of our circumstances for His good purposes.

Learning about monetary issues faced by Dada was important for me. He had a large family and lived on a small stipend. Grandma played her helper's role beautifully by sewing clothes for her own children and for her neighbours and selling buffalo milk to raise money to feed the family. When younger, Grandma had been keen to learn to sew, knit and crochet, and made a request to be trained in these skills. So she was sent to a special school to be taught these things.

Just as Eve was given the role of helper (Genesis 2:18-24), I also have tried to fulfil this role to the best of my ability. It was important for me to learn about managing finances and budgeting for the benefit of the family. I learned we are only stewards of our money and we will be answerable for it all to the Mighty Giver.

I knew that I needed to hear about other people's experiences and listen to their wisdom to sustain my marriage relationship; I needed to understand my own likes, my dislikes, who I am, the purpose of my life – and my focus needed to be on the bigger picture. I understood that we grow and change with time; I needed to grow in love and knowledge of God to understand human relationships better.

It is often said that we cannot change the other person; we need to change ourselves first. For example, choosing to live in love and peace, choosing not to break communication and not letting the 'sun go down' on anger (Ephesians 4:26) without apologising and making up: this is what the Bible commands me to do! Jesus said, 'A new command I give you: love one another. As I have loved you, so you must love one another' (John 13:34), and the whole of 1 Corinthians 13 explains that the greatest of all things is love (v13)! Ephesians 5:25 states, 'Husbands, love your wives, just as Christ loved the church', and verse 28 carries on to say, 'husbands ought to love their wives as their own bodies'. I live in hope that the seeds of the Word will continue to sprout in my journey of grace.

2

Sprouting Seeds

When I was six years old, in 1958, my mother was taken ill with tuberculosis (TB) while pregnant with her sixth child. My father was not happy with her for not telling him earlier about this illness and took her straight to Sialkot Mission Hospital, which was more than four hours away from Faisalabad. All five of us children were sent back to Faisalabad to live with our grandparents and uncles and aunts in the vicarage. Our father returned to Haripur Hazara for his job and visited us during his holidays.

While I missed my parents greatly, I look back with great fondness at this time of living with my grandparents, appreciating what a privilege it was to be growing up in the vicarage and witnessing Dada's spiritual discipline and dedicated ministry. We received immense love and care from aunts and uncles. The vicarage was surrounded with all kinds of native fruit trees, which we were privileged to enjoy. There was also a swing attached to a large tree, which we spent many hours sharing with our cousins during their school holidays. I learned recently that the vicarage was demolished a few years ago and now a modern church building, with the capacity to hold 5,000 people, stands on the site!

Having one buffalo on the property back then, Dada grew a field of green corn around the vicarage grounds for the buffalo to eat, and we enjoyed fresh milk, butter and *lassi* (a kind of yoghurt drink). There was an old-fashioned hand-driven cutter to cut the greens for the buffalo, which a house maid first had to cut from the field and then chop finely.

I have strong, happy memories of playing for hours in the shade of the trees with our cousins and neighbours' children. Extended families all living together seems a thing of the past, but I remember its great value and warmth, where everyone lived in peace and harmony, and where love and respect was given and received by all.

During the school holidays, our aunts and their children visited us, and big pots of food were cooked by my grandmother on the homemade wood burner, which was common practice at that time. *Chapatis*, flatbreads, were cooked in a clay tandoor oven, also heated by a wooden fire, and then shared around the big dining table. Men of the household were not expected to help with cooking or washing up – this was typical of the Asian culture of that time!

My fondest memory was that of walking with Dada to church. Every Sunday he would bring back and forth a large clock from the church wall for safekeeping at home. We enjoyed Sunday school, which was led by our youngest aunt, and learned a lot of the Scriptures and Old Testament stories. The class consisted of about thirty children, most of whom continued to hold to the Christian faith and did well in later life.

Our grandmother was a hardworking woman. Having raised seven children of her own, she now had the task of taking on the five of us. She worked hard in the kitchen with the help of the live-in housemaid. Our grandmother was a woman of faith who was fully involved in church life, leading the church choir on Sundays. Our bedtime stories included Bible stories and moral tales that I still remember to this day.

I always benefited from Grandma's stories about what life was like in the past, even before Partition. I wished that she might always stay with us. She lived to see me leaving for the UK and died a few years later. I will always treasure her empathy and help in many ways.

Our evening family prayers were held in the open air, in the courtyard of the vicarage, with my uncles and aunts present and led by Dada. These times have left a great impression on me. We sang a psalm, read part of the Scriptures and Dada would share a short message before asking one of us to pray.

Once during such a family prayer time, in the vicarage courtyard, I remember the unforgettable sound of the flapping of wings, like that of a big bird passing over the vicarage. This was explained by our aunt as an angel of protection that passed by each night. My sister told me that after Dada's retirement, in the new house, when we went to sleep on the rooftop, she also heard the sound of flapping wings. Upon asking Dada, she was told that it was the angel of protection who passed over every night. For her this memory has always been comforting, no matter what she has gone through in life.

Another incident I can vividly recall, and one which we can all laugh about now, was that during an evening prayer time my younger sister saw a cat coming and started to scream. The rest of us automatically started to scream as well and that was the end of Dada's prayer time!

One autumn morning, Dada took me to visit my mother in the hospital in Sialkot. It was a large ward with many beds spread out in it, as is necessary with TB. I don't remember coming too close to her, yet I will always remember that scene. It would prove to be the last time I saw her face. I will always be grateful to Dada for taking me to see her. It was after the birth of my brother, the sixth sibling, and I remember my mother saying to me, 'I am getting better now and soon will come home.' Yet in the same year of 1958, on Christmas morning when our new clothes were being ironed for church, a telegram arrived from the hospital telling us that our mother had died earlier that morning.

I sensed from the whispers what had happened without even being told of the contents of the telegram. That day, no one apart from Dada went to church, and after the service the flow of people started coming with their condolences, which is very much part of our cultural tradition. This can continue for many weeks after someone has passed away.

It must have been on the second visit after the death of my mother that my maternal grandad announced, 'Our daughter has died now and we will have nothing to do with your family from now on.' I assume it may have been because of family tensions but I was too young to know the reason. We did not meet again for many years.

Our mother was buried in the city of Sialkot graveyard. My father, his brother, both grandfathers, along with my elder aunt, all went to bury her, and on their return my aunt hugged me and cried out loud, saying, 'We have buried your mother under tons of earth.' That was the only verbal confirmation given to me as to what had just taken place.

Soon after this, my life went back to so-called 'normal'. It was decided that the newborn baby boy be given up for adoption. The reason could have been that it was too much for our grandmother to cope with, as she already had the five of us to bring up! Alternatively, there could have been fears as to whether my mother's TB would have had a negative impact on his future health. We did meet him again much later on, when he was married and had his own family. He looked healthy and happy with no such issues.

Our uncles and aunts gave us the best love anyone could give. We enjoyed their wedding ceremonies. When my aunts and uncles got married and started having children, I innocently thought, 'It is always only after the wedding ceremony that they start having babies. It must be an answer to the prayers offered at the wedding ceremony.' Now I smile about this and tell it as one of my embarrassing stories.

I was one of the flower girls at my uncle's wedding, along with my cousin. After seeing them, a young, happy couple, the thought of mortality crossed my mind that they would have to die one day as well. I must have been eight years of age. I began to realise that we all have to die one day, and I thought, 'That means it's not worth doing anything in this world.'

I carried on pondering these questions. Slowly but surely, from Sunday school teaching and learning from the Scriptures, the purpose of life became clear. I understood that God's love shown to the world in Jesus Christ has given me assurance that death has no hold on me, and that after death I will live with Jesus forever, because of His sacrifice on the cross for me, His blood being sufficient to cleanse me of my sins.

I must have been about nine years old, three years after my mother died, when I began to realise that this whole experience of being raised without your own mother present was not a natural one. This seemed a rough start to life, and I always felt a kind of emptiness inside. Maybe this has left me with a sense of apprehension in life, as though something important is missing. It caused me to grow up quickly, and my prayers always go out for the children of the world that they may grow up in secure and loving homes.

While my cousins had their mothers with them, the recurring question as to why this had to happen to me often crossed my mind.

I have grown up not knowing what a mother's love is like. Mothering Sunday has always involved mixed feelings for me, not really being able to relate fully to having a mother, although our stepmother tried her best to play her role. Yet now, through my relationship with my own children, I feel I can enter more into this day of celebration. Also, my Christian faith reassures me that God is both my Mother and my Father. He loves me way more than my earthly mother could ever love (Isaiah 49:15) and can fill all the gaps in my life. I know that He has always been there for me, no matter what I have gone through in the past.

Being the eldest child, I was expected to behave well, to do well in life and to be a role model to my younger siblings. Though I failed many times, in God's grace He was present at every step to pick me up again.

My primary school education was at a church school, where my life was enriched with daily assemblies and a period of Christian studies. All the teachers were of the Christian faith, and I was often asked to tell Bible stories in front of the class. Unlike in recent years, the Muslim students had no objections to learning the Scriptures with us.

One end-of-year results day, the speech from the head of the school left a great impression on me. She said something about our results being according to the work we had done throughout the year, and nothing could be changed now. The thought of potentially not doing well worried me and I made a promise to myself that from the next year I would work hard all year round! I was relieved to hear that I had passed my exams and I kept the promise to always work hard in the future. From that incident, I learned that our life is not about experiencing individual separate events and then just forgetting the past; rather, all life events are interconnected, and God has intended for us to live life as a whole and to complete the journey.

My school was about a kilometre away from home. The thought of walking alone back and forth scares me now, but it was much safer to do so back then. Later, when attending high school, I remember commuting along with other students in a simple horse-drawn carriage, known as a *tonga*. That led to some fun incidents! Sometimes the horse tripped and the people in the front had no safety bar to hold on to or seatbelts to wear, so they tipped forward. Conversely, the people at the back went up into the air! Thinking back, it was actually quite scary, but that was the most common and economical way of commuting at that time.

It was becoming difficult for grandmother to take care of us. About four years after my mother died, at the insistence of Dada, my father remarried – I was about ten at the time. He and his new wife settled back in Haripur Hazara with my three younger siblings, leaving me and my sister with our grandparents. We visited them in the summer holidays with Dada and were accompanied by our cousins from Lahore. This is where I remember our aunt teaching us a short prayer to say before eating food. We have all remembered it and have passed it on to our grandchildren as well.

I have lasting memories of distant hills facing our housing development, and pleasant weather with a cool breeze in the hot summers. Haripur Hazara is also known for being the birthplace of our former president, Ayyub Khan.

The memories of this place, the calm and pleasant atmosphere, the playtime with friends, are very fresh in my mind. Our house had a large front garden, where my father nurtured his interest in gardening and had a vegetable patch, and on our visits we enjoyed organic vegetables and fresh fruits. The closer side of the house had pretty, colourful flowers growing there.

My grandmother and aunts inspired me to sew and knit. We had to wear knitted cardigans, and that encouraged me learn to knit for myself and for my siblings as well. Most of my cooking skills and tips came from my father, who cooked for us and gave us helpful hints. And when I developed a passion for gardening, I could easily give credit for it to my father's influence – without realising at that time how important this seed analogy would become; it was going to be part of my faith.

3
Established Plants

Dada retired in 1961 after serving as a priest at the main United Presbyterian Church in Faisalabad where all four of his daughters, as well as I and all my five sisters, were christened, confirmed and married. His retiring farewell function was in my church school grounds. It was a well-attended event. I remember garlands of fresh flowers around his neck. After others made speeches appreciating his commitment to serve, Dada made a final speech thanking God for His calling and for sustaining him for all those years. He thanked the elders and all the other co-workers in Christ and also thanked God for the retirement home that he had been able to build with God's grace in a nearby area in Faisalabad.

My father arranged for his job to be transferred to Faisalabad so the whole family could live together with my grandparents, because as the older son he felt a sense of duty to be with his parents in their old age. All of us lived together; the house had five reasonably large rooms, but there were many adjustments to be made as they settled into their new home. It was like a new beginning for all of us.

Three more siblings would be added to my family in the coming years. Having new babies around was a source of great joy to us all and we enjoyed helping to raise them. One of my cousins was very much part of our lives, and it was a joy to have her around and see her grow; her parents lived with us before moving upstairs. In the summer months we slept on the rooftop, with mosquito nets. After his family moved to the upstairs part of the house with his wife and daughter, we began to sleep on their rooftop in the open air during the summer months. On occasions there would be sharp showers or high winds and we would run downstairs, leaving the bedding folded in the room upstairs. This disturbed sleep did not help when getting up for school in the morning! But this was another fun time I treasure from my childhood. In the summer evenings, after the sunset, the rooftop was our relaxation area. We often went up there to enjoy the cooler air and to look out at the fast-developing area around us. The rooftop was also a good place to sit out in the sun in the winter months, and to enjoy eating oranges, guavas and carrots.

We were one of very few Christian families in the area, but it was such a peaceful and friendly neighbourhood that we never felt unsafe or threatened; instead we were accepted as one of the communities and were known as the Christian priest's family.

Our stepmother, my father's new wife, had her hands full, generously taking care of the five of us as well as raising our stepbrother and two stepsisters. She was an early riser; the first thing she did was to unlock the main door of the house, and to lock it again was the last thing she did at night, although none of us ever thought of it as being a dangerous or unsafe area.

Owning a buffalo, her early morning job was to mix the curd with a manual wooden mixer operated with ropes wound around it (these days modern electric mixers are used!). The curd was set the night before in a large earthen pot. My duty was to gather the newly formed white butter (called *makhan*) from the resulting *lassi*, having to scrape it off the wooden mixer as well. This butter was to go on our breakfast *chapatis*, or *parathas* (a different type of flatbread), prepared by our stepmother. She was a hard-working and efficient woman who liked to do the jobs in a meticulous way, and taught us to do the same. Her idea was to train us well for our future married lives. She kept a good eye on all of us. We girls were to dress modestly, without make-up or jewellery.

Our father provided for all the family, which was no easy feat with such a large number of children to take care of. He used to buy enough fabric for all of us to have our school uniforms sewed together at home.

Pakistan is a dry and dusty country with four seasons, and the houses need cleaning on a daily basis. We often helped out in this work, giving us good training for the future in terms of tidiness and general organisation. Every weekend each one of us had to clean and tidy our own shared rooms and wash our school uniforms and other clothes and bedding when needed. There were no washing machines back then for us! Top-loading manual washing machines were introduced eventually; ones that could be wheeled close to our water supply. The automatic ones followed much later.

Our evening family prayer times continued; as soon as we had finished our supper, Dada would call everyone together, saying, 'Children, bring the hymn books and the Bible.' We all sat around on small homemade wooden steps or on the portable *char pies* (beds) where we sang a psalm/hymn. Then, being the eldest grandchild, I was asked to read a part of the Scriptures, which Dada then explained. Either I or one of the adults was then asked to pray, or Dada himself prayed. He would name the needs of each family member individually. Later in life he would keep in close touch with all his children via letter-writing. This is something I have been inspired to do – I keep in close contact with my family members this way.

The family worship times had a great impact on my life and gave me a long-lasting and solid foundation in the Christian faith. I soon learned that when Dada asked us questions about God, an answer of 'Jesus' was never wrong! The basic seeds of the good news of Jesus Christ were sown and watered well. This simple faith, ingrained in me from childhood and in the years to come, continued to grow and mature towards a fruitful harvest. I must add that I always felt that a little bit 'different' within myself, although I wasn't someone who would compare myself to anyone else, though I did not know that this had anything to do with God at that time.

One particular verse, Hebrews 9:12, has stayed in my mind from Dada's teaching up to this very day, with his voice and words in Urdu: 'He did not enter by the means of the blood of goats and calves; but he entered the Most Holy Place once for all by his own blood, so obtaining eternal redemption.' He spoke gently and humbly and with such great conviction, it began to ingrain Christian faith and life within me. Dada would speak of his Christian conversion in this family time as well, which did not seem of much significance to me then, until I heard about other people's conversions and the difference that Christ had made in their lives. Much later on, my own experience of meeting the living Christ brought the whole story alive.

I was tempted to ask him if he had actually seen God, but then I thought it would be embarrassing for him to answer me if he hadn't! I did not like to embarrass him. Much later from his life and service I understood that Dada had seen God with his spiritual eyes when God touched his heart and he believed in Him.

My siblings and I joined the local state junior school and made some good Muslim friends. My sisters and I were the only Christian girls there, and apart from two Christian teachers, the staff were Muslims. The day began with school assembly, with the reciting of the set verses from the Quran, called Tilawat, by a member of staff. Unconsciously we learned the whole passage by heart. I was often asked by other girls, 'Why don't you convert to Islam?' In return my quick answer was, 'Why don't you convert to Christianity?' They had no answer. I would be in trouble if I said this today, but society was much more tolerant of different religions back then. Only once there was an issue: while at school, I was drinking water from a tap. Some girls came and confronted me for using the same tap that they used. However, straight away, my other friends came to support me and told these girls off, warning them not to do that again.

I often turned to Dada for help with my English grammar homework, and for help with maths I turned to

41

one of my aunties during her holidays on her summer break from school, where she taught. One of my uncles, who was a mathematician, was also a great help when visiting from the break from school. My father, Emmanuel, was always serious about our education, along with our general health. He would give us extra vitamins and minerals, alongside a good diet, fresh milk from our one buffalo and fresh eggs from our chickens. Our stepmother taught maths and English from home for neighbouring children, to assist with the family finances.

To encourage us in our studies, Dada would give us a cash gift if we got overall marks of more than 60 per cent in our school exams, otherwise we did not get anything. He also paid for both of our brothers to be educated in a private Christian school. One was my natural brother and the other was my stepbrother. We girls were not afforded this honour! This is a cultural mindset, according to which, since girls will be married off and will become a part of a different family, there is not much need to spend a lot on their education. Boys, on the other hand, are the ones who carry the family line forward, and therefore need better education.

In one of our summer holidays, Dada decided to treat all the grandchildren to a trip to Lahore for a week to visit the historical places there. Lahore is known as the cultural centre of the country. There are a lot of historical places from the time of the Mughal and British Empires. We stayed at our aunt's place. Her son, our cousin, accompanied us as our guide. The historical places were amazing to visit, and learning the history was helpful for our education. The highlight of the holiday was a visit to the zoo where we enjoyed riding on the back of an elephant!

The home atmosphere, the method and the style of running the household were all great examples to me. The lessons we learned could be incorporated into our own family settings later in life.

When I was older, aged twelve, I attended a government high school that required a long journey each day. Sadly, in the first summer break I was taken ill and ended up missing the rest of the academic year, owing to constant visits to the hospital. My symptoms were a high fever that developed into a constant chesty cough. Dada took me for my hospital appointments on his pushbike, with me perched on the back. Lots of prayers were offered for my healing, along with me being given many different medicines, which seem to have caused an imbalance to my hormonal system.

Dada told me that he was praying with tears every day for my healing, and I believe that God was bringing lots of good out of this long illness, as it was a time for me to reflect on my life. Through it I learned to trust in His healing power through prayer, and also to appreciate the love and care I received from everyone.

One rather strange incident that happened during this time was when accompanying my stepmother on a visit to her home town. We were on the bus home when I felt myself go into some sort of a trance, and I began chanting loudly, so that all the bus could hear. My words were, 'My Jesus, living Jesus.' I was swaying from side to side, repeating the same words over and over again. Nobody in the bus said anything to me to make me stop.

Years later, my stepmother, reflecting on the incident, said to me, 'You really gave glory to Jesus on the bus that day.' As for me, I'm not sure exactly what happened. Was it the Holy Spirit moving me? I can't say for sure, but it certainly isn't something I will ever forget!

After a long time away from school, I made a promise to myself that I would in future approach all things wholeheartedly and with great patience. The image I had was that of tying a ribbon in a neat bow. I was fully recovered by the beginning of the next academic year, but did not return to the government school; instead I attended the local middle school. I must say that I felt energised and refreshed. It was like a new beginning. I also started doing a lot better in class! My academic grades were greatly improved, and I was reminded of the verse in Colossians where it says, 'Whatever you do, work at it with all your heart, as working for the Lord, not for human masters' (Colossians 3:23). Surprisingly, I did so well that I was only a few marks away from getting a scholarship!

I went on to study at a government college for women in Faisalabad, doing a Bachelor of Arts (BA) degree. Initially I studied science, but found it wasn't for me, so I switched to the Arts, which my father suggested could be used later for a career in teaching. At that time, unlike today, teaching and nursing were the only professions available to women as a career.

While I was in my third year of my BA degree exams, aged twenty-one, Dada was taken ill. He was admitted to hospital for breathing issues, but insisted on coming back home. During this time, most of his children were able to visit him. He told them, 'I have a few more days to go. You did not have to come so early!' On the evening of 10th

November 1972, while his whole family were gathered there, he got up from his bed and sat on the settee to pray, as was his custom. His prayer seemed assured and powerful with no sign of any weakness. After reciting the Lord's Prayer, he got up, with my dad's help, walked to the mantelpiece to put his glasses away and then walked back to his bed to lie down to sleep. His breathing was calming down as if he was breathing normally. My aunt said, 'He is getting better,' but within a few seconds we noticed his breathing starting to fade, and then he breathed his last.

According to tradition, his body was kept in our front room for the night, accompanied by his sons, who took turns staying with him. The body was prepared for the funeral and the service was then held in the courtyard of the house. This was the common practice of the day.

This was my first experience of witnessing a death. I could not help crying aloud, and in that moment I uttered, 'Who is going to lead our prayers now?' Inside I kept praying, 'Please, Lord, make him wake up!' This second loss, after that of my mother, had a lasting impact on my life. Especially the final moments, when Dada was faithful to his last breath.

Life is full of surprises. It's very hard to predict from one year to another. I needed to wait to see what was in store for me next.

4
Budding

I was twenty-one years old and we were just about recovering from Dada's death. I was in my second year of final degree exams – altogether, I had to study four years in college – when a proposal of marriage was brought to my father by my mother's elder sister, who was a nursing sister at Lahore's Mayo Hospital. Prior to this she told me that one of her colleagues had already met me and remembered me when I was five years old and had visited Lahore with my aunt who was serving as a staff nurse there. My younger sister had also recently joined the nursing profession at the same hospital, and now this nursing sister was asking for my hand in marriage for her son Stanley who was in the UK. When my aunt asked if she wanted to meet our family before proceeding, she answered, 'I have met you all and know you well; that is sufficient for me for the engagement to go ahead.' I was speechless and waited for my father's decision.

This news gave my father a huge fright! He said, 'She is still studying,' but my aunt responded, 'She can continue with her studies. Stanley's family will come to visit you, both families can meet each other, and Amelia

and Stanley can get engaged when Stanley visits later on.'
My father agreed to this and visited Stanley's family in
Lahore where they swapped photographs of me and
Stanley, and then the date for their visit was set for some
time in March 1973. It was just a visit for the families to get
to know each other better – so we thought.

All the arrangements were made, and food was
prepared to welcome the family. As they arrived at the
house, I was given several gifts along with an engagement
ring! What we thought was a casual visit turned out to be
my engagement! To this day I cannot understand where
the misunderstanding had occurred, but I accepted it as
God's will for me, even though I had not even met Stanley
face to face at that stage! I had already made up my mind
beforehand not to choose a partner for myself, in case I
made a wrong choice.

Some readers, especially in the West, may find the idea
of 'arranged marriage' very foreign or even troubling. I
can sympathise with them. The idea that someone else
decides who you will spend the rest of your life with – a
person you may not even have met – seems scary.
However, in most of human history, that is how marriages
were done! In my culture, all marriages were arranged. Of
course, I felt odd, since everything happened so quickly,
and Stanley was not even there when his mother asked for
my hand in marriage. But I felt that I had nothing to say
since, at that time, children were not allowed to question
parents' choices in these matters. I had even seen some
weddings without the groom being present. People would
put the picture of the groom next to the bride and do the
wedding!

Anyway, I was officially engaged, with a ring on my finger. It felt good in some ways. My college friends were shocked and made funny jokes. Stanley must have felt the same, but in obedience to his mother agreed to the arrangement. He asked through his mother if he could write to me. My father permitted this, so I needed to buy airmail envelopes and a letter-writing pad, but I had no money, and I was reluctant to ask my father, as I was not in the habit of asking for money from my father even for my educational needs. My sister, who was in the same college as I was, would make such requests for the both of us when required.

I was a bit concerned about where to find the money for the envelopes but kept the need to myself. On that same day, in the evening, one of my aunts who lived close by came to visit me with her friend who had come to congratulate me on my engagement, and she gave me a gift of five rupees, which was enough to buy a writing pad and a pack of international envelopes with some leftover change as well! God had provided in my time of need. This was beyond my expectation and increased my faith in His care for me. I took this provision as a positive sign of God's approval of my engagement. I was learning to understand that God is interested even in the smallest things in my life.

After the engagement, I gave up the idea of taking my final-year degree exams, thinking that the degree would not be recognised in the UK anyway. When Stanley heard of this, he sent a message through his mother to convince me to take them, but I would not listen! Finally, Stanley convinced me personally to do so, writing in his letter that I had studied hard for my final degree exam and all that work would be wasted. He said that he could wait till after my exams before coming over to marry me.

Looking back, I am happy that I listened and finished my degree, as it was a milestone in my education and something that gave me confidence for future studies. It was not easy, however, as, owing to political unrest, my exams were brought forward by three months. It was a huge challenge for me to revise two years' work in such a short time, and on top of it all, I aimed to pass all the subjects first time round. I revised day and night, getting up early in the morning and sleeping for only a few hours. I took this challenge very seriously and did it with all my heart.

At times I was quite stressed out and even needed to go to the doctor for medication as I was having heart palpitations. During my revision, I came across the exact type of guiding materials that I needed, which were a tremendous help to me, and I found that most of the exam questions were in line with what I had revised. At times it felt like my pen was just writing on its own! The whole episode made me strong and confident. My faith grew in God's provision; it was a small step of faith that I had taken and God continued to build upon it. The main point is that once I put my hand in His, He did not let it go and guided me through every step of my life.

Stanley and I continued to communicate via letter. It took one week for the post to reach Manchester and then another week for his reply to come back to me in Faisalabad.

Through our letters, Stanley proposed that I should start looking for a job one month after my arrival in the UK to contribute towards our living costs in the UK. There was not much in our letters about plans for our future married life, though, such as where we would live. So I kept all such thoughts to myself. I had not worked before so this would be my first-ever job. In Pakistan the only professional career I could have pursued was that of a teacher. In the UK, however, to be a teacher would require a further two years of study – plus my English needed much improvement first!

Stanley's mother often spoke to my aunt. She would talk about how hard Stanley was working, studying in the morning and working in the evening, trying hard to build a life in the UK. Also, she talked about his siblings, four older brothers and two younger sisters settled in Lahore.

During this time, Stanley's mother was taken ill with gallstones. They went ahead with an operation but found that they could not proceed, as they discovered that she had developed cancer. Stanley arrived in Lahore for our marriage, nine months after the engagement, and was met with this very difficult situation.

He visited us in Faisalabad and met us all for the first time. He was the same person with the same personality as he is to this day! He never spoke about his worries, but rather worked them out in his own mind and found a way to deal with them. He always kept a positive attitude. Preparations for the wedding were not a big stress to him; he took everything in his stride. He never loses sleep because of worries and anxiety. He speaks his mind without too much forethought and works hard to achieve his goals.

Entering into this new relationship was a big change for me. I was a quiet person with few words, whereas Stanley was 'loud'. I realised that we were very different people and that there was a lot for us to learn about each other. But I had been engaged now for nine months and there was no room for second thoughts!

My degree results were announced in Lahore, as our college fell under the Lahore Examination Board, so Stanley collected them along with my cousin, because at that time Stanley was in his home town of Lahore and I was in my home town of Faisalabad. I had passed all my subjects! It was a great relief to know that my heart's desire had happened.

The wedding date was initially set for 17th December 1973 but had to be postponed owing to the declining condition of Stanley's mother. I visited her in the hospital and she congratulated me on my exam results. I replied, 'I made it because of your sincere prayers.' She was happy to hear this. During her time in hospital, my aunt visited her almost daily, just to be with her and support her. It was a great sacrifice on her part to do so, as the hospital was some distance from her home. Stanley's mother died in the early hours of 26th December 1973. My father went to Lahore for the funeral service.

A few days afterwards, the question of the wedding date was discussed again. Stanley's family wanted to postpone the marriage to a much later date, suggesting that Stanley return to the UK first. But my father threatened, 'If it is postponed till another time, there will not be any marriage.' The date was set for 31st December of the same year, just a few days after Stanley's mother's death.

The marriage ceremony itself was a simple affair in our family's United Presbyterian Church with just family and close friends present, followed by a traditional lunch and cake-cutting ceremony. Because of her ill health, Stanley's mother had not been able to make any preparations for the wedding, so her younger sister and her husband had taken over the arrangements. We were grateful for all their generosity and hospitality.

Our marriage was quite unlike the usual traditional marriages of the day – owing to the recent death of Stanley's mother, the wedding was simpler and more subdued. For example, my father cancelled the musicians who would normally accompany the groom's party. My aunty, however, got a few dresses made for me to wear in the days following the wedding. A few eyebrows were raised at the lack of traditional preparations, but these things did not matter to me, as I took to heart the vows we made during the wedding, to care for each other for richer or for poorer!

This experience taught me many things. One was that jewellery is not for me to own. I tend to lose what little I already have anyway! Traditionally, a full set or more of gold jewellery and bangles, as many or as heavy in weight as a family can afford, is given to the bride. But because the arrangements for our wedding were made at such short notice, jewellery was not a part of it.

I have never missed having such jewellery in England as it is not so commonly worn here. As it says in the Scriptures, 'Your beauty should not come from outward adornment, such as elaborate hairstyles and the wearing of gold jewellery or fine clothes. Rather, it should be that of your inner self, the unfading beauty of a gentle and quiet spirit, which is of great worth in God's sight' (1 Peter 3:3-4). Many years later Stanley bought me a few sets of gold jewellery to make up for those that I had missed out on at the time.

After the wedding, Stanley and I could not stay in Stanley's family home. Instead we stayed with their neighbours and good friends for about three weeks. Their daughter gave us her room. During this time, we visited most of our relatives in various towns in Pakistan. Shortly afterwards, Stanley had to return to the UK for work. I was supposed to join him as soon as my visa was granted. I stayed with my parents with so many questions on my mind and with no idea of how long this wait would be..

5
Waiting

I believe that waiting goes against our human nature, especially in this digital age. Microwave ovens have made us impatient to wait even two minutes for food to get reheated, compared to the time taken to light a fire or reheat on the hob! We often prefer to drive even short distances rather than walk for a bit of exercise. Mobile phones have brought the world to our fingertips. The whole world is available to us through the internet, and we have come to depend and rely upon it so much. Sometimes even more than our reliance upon God! It has replaced our dictionary, concordance and newspapers as well. It is our watch, alarm clock and map. It is said that the world has become closer to us, but in contrast our family members sitting right beside us may be further away.

Instead of going to the bank, we use online banking. Walking to the shops may seem like a waste of time for us; rather, we order a home delivery. Technology has caused us to become dependent on it, so much so that we feel lost if we spend a day without it! When I was growing up we had a simple life with few gadgets to work with. We had fewer bills to worry about, and ate simple, homemade food. Although there was plenty of hard, physical work, I think we had less mental stress and resulting health issues. Having said all this, the recent coronavirus epidemic has forced us to take a step back and take stock of things. God can use even terrible circumstances to draw us closer to Him.

I had to come back to Faisalabad to my father's house to stay until my UK visa was granted, so that I could join Stanley there. I had to wait one year for the visa, but it seemed like an eternity, especially as I had a good deal of apprehension over my future. Still, I had no option other than to wait. It was bearable as my family were very supportive; especially my grandmother, who felt sorry for me for being left in this situation. Also, Stanley was supporting me financially during this time. Sadly, our community was not always as helpful, though, and was quick to make negative assumptions, such as, 'Stanley is not going to call you from the UK; he just married you because of his mother's wishes!' The worst one was, 'He might be interested in someone else there, or might have a family there as well!' Overall, it felt like a wasted year of my life.

In this time of waiting, I kept myself busy with housework, learning new skills in cooking and generally how to run a home. But I was faced with disappointment. I was not granted the visa. Some of the necessary papers were delayed in the post from England and so I was given another date some six months further away! That was a frustrating time for me. I could have been in England starting my new married life with Stanley, but who can know the mind of God? He had a much bigger and much better plan for me than my short-sighted thinking.

I came to a point of hopelessness. Tired of waiting, I decided in my heart, 'I am not bothered any more whether I am granted the visa or not. I will simply go for further studies, train to be a teacher and make my life here in Pakistan.'

During this long time of waiting, I joined a typing school, where I learned to use a manual typewriter, which felt quite exciting and was also helpful in typing letters to Stanley! When Stanley came to know about my visa issues, he chose to pursue another option, which was to apply for a British passport for me via the British Embassy in Islamabad. This option of getting a British passport while still in Pakistan, in order to travel to the UK for the first time, seemed like a real blessing and privilege to me. This gave me some new hope, but it still involved another three months of waiting!

Stanley had come to Britain in 1961 at the age of eleven, accompanied by a family friend. He stayed for three years as a student and went back to Pakistan. He then returned to the UK in 1966 as a returning resident and obtained a British passport. I could therefore join him after our marriage.

In retrospect, I believe this extra time of waiting on top of the year that had already passed was used by God so that I might experience the grace of our Lord Jesus and receive guidance and wisdom for the future. I was prompted to turn to the Scriptures, and while reading these I was filled with peace and a sense of calm, no longer anxious about all the waiting. My stepmother observed me reading the Bible and made the comment, 'Amelia is reading the Bible with full commitment and dedication and God is going to bless her through this!' She had been born and brought up in a Christian home, but, despite this comment, had not yet received Jesus as her Saviour. Maybe my reading the Bible prompted her to read and get closer to God in a committed way.

I came to know later that sometime after I left Pakistan, she accepted Jesus as her personal Lord and Saviour, received the believer's baptism and became a God-loving and prayerful person, fasting regularly during the time of Lent, and was blessed with prophetic gifts. She used these gifts to talk to people about Jesus and encourage them in their faith. She had the courage to tell them if something in their life was not in accord with what the Bible said. The outlook of her life had completely changed when she had to take care of us, but one could see that she was happier, fulfilled, appreciative of what we meant to her, and she became a blessing to all of us. She understood and experienced clearly and deeply the love of God, and shared this with us in return.

She told us once that she had had a dream in which Dada put a hosepipe in her hand, sprinkling fresh water all around. She took this to mean that she should carry on his work of telling others about Jesus. She would hence share the gospel with visitors and all the people she met.

In the time of waiting, I spent long hours reading and meditating on the Scriptures and various verses came alive to me, talking about the issues of family life and teaching me that I needed to be a godly mother for my children, leading them in His ways. And for Stanley, Proverbs 31:23 came to my mind: 'Her husband is respected at the city gate, where he takes his seat among the elders of the land.' The message I understood from this verse was that it should be one of my responsibilities to give Stanley respect and to support him as he became a respected member of the community. In fact, as a cultural mark of respect, I had only recently started calling him by his first name, choosing previously to use the formal rather than personal version of address. Another culturally appropriate way of addressing your husband would be to call them your child's father!

For me personally it was the rest of Proverbs 31 that really struck me and which I took to heart. It talks of how the woman is to be hard-working for her family. I also read in Genesis 2 that the woman was to be her partner's helper. Being a helper does not imply lesser value in the Bible, God Himself being called the helper of His people.[2] I needed to work hard and to assist Stanley in whatever ways we needed to build our married life together.

The parable of the wise man building his house upon the rock in Matthew 7:24-25 also spoke to me, giving me assurance that our house would be built on the rock of Jesus, and that if we built our marriage upon that rock then He would promise to protect us, whatever may come. Actually, I also learned a lot from my father and stepmother, seeing how hard they worked together, bringing us up to be well-rounded adults.

After this time spent with God, reading and meditating on His Word, I received peace in my heart. The worry over my visa and time 'wasted' seemed to vanish. I realised that perhaps this was all part of God's purpose for my life at this stage. The foundation was built upon God and the

---

[2] See for example Psalm 46:1.

journey was about to begin with the assurance of Jesus, that He would hold my hand to lead me onwards into this new life. Within three months I received a letter from the British Embassy in Islamabad asking me to come to collect my British nationality certificate and to apply for my British passport as well. This meant that at last I could travel to the UK on a British passport. Stanley subsequently organised my travel to the UK.

There was a pastor who worked for Campus Crusade and used to visit us for prayers and to support my siblings in their faith. During one such visit he asked me, 'How are you planning to serve God in the UK?'

I was speechless and after a pause I replied, 'I don't know!' and it was left at that. Actually, he stayed with us when he first came to the UK, before continuing on his way to east London to begin his ministry there.

I noted that God did not rush me when He brought me to a foreign land. He did not ask of me more than I could bear. He is a loving and patient God who gave me plenty of time to settle before he assigned specific responsibilities to me. He prepared and strengthened me so that all the glory would go to Him.

Well, the time came for me to take the first step. My flight was booked for 11th May 1975. It was two days before my twenty-third birthday, and I was glad to be able to celebrate this with Stanley, to mark the beginning of my new life with him. All my family were sad to let me go so far away, but they promised to keep in touch through letters, as we did not have a phone line in the house in Faisalabad until a little later on and so had to go to our neighbour's house to receive phone calls.

I was sent on my way with their best wishes and prayers. Before travelling to London, I visited Lahore to say goodbye to Stanley's family. My cousin always accompanied me while I was in Lahore. It was very generous of him to take time off from work every time I visited there.

While in Lahore I decided to visit Stanley's mother's grave to pay my respects, but unfortunately I was not able to trace the exact site. I decided to get a memorial plaque made for her; again, my cousin helped me with this matter. This pleased Stanley, and he was grateful to me for being so thoughtful.

On visiting one of his brother's houses, I was warned that Stanley was not going to receive any inheritance from his father's property, because he was a British national now! These words made me think and I decided in my heart that on my arrival I would need to enquire about how we could go about buying a house of our own in the UK, and so securing a future for our children.

I was leaving home for the first time to go thousands of miles away to meet a man I hardly knew, but still I was looking forward to experiencing this new life that God was laying before me. It was a time of mixed emotions for me, for I was also sad to leave my home, family and culture and to adopt a new culture, one that would be totally foreign to me.

I left everyone with tears in my eyes and began my journey to the UK by initially travelling to Lahore. I did not know when or where I would see my family again, or how long it would be before I would be able to return to Pakistan. I was also apprehensive about flying for the first time and having to do this alone, not knowing anything about airports or boarding passes and the like. My father, however, accompanied me to Allama Iqbal International Airport Lahore to see me safely onto the flight to Karachi, where I was then to catch an international flight for London. My cousin, my aunt and my sister also accompanied us to the airport.

My stepmother had already told me that she had two cousin brothers living in London with their families and she had contacted them to take care of me. They had promised that as I would be new to the country, they would be like my family in the UK (and indeed they kept their promise).

My father did not easily show his emotions, but I could see the sadness on his face. He demonstrated his practical concern for my safety when he requested his sister, my aunt, to meet me at the other end of the flight, for which she had had to travel from Hyderabad to Karachi.

I coped well on the flight as the airport staff and the crew were very helpful. Upon landing, I met my aunt, accompanied by my cousin, and one of their good friends who had driven them to Karachi. It was generous of my aunt to take this time with me. I remember that she took me to a Chinese restaurant, situated inside the airport building, my first experience of such food, as it was not common in Pakistan at that time. A few hours later, she saw me off for my international flight to London. I was full of questions about what London looked like in spring, what sort of life I would find in my new home, what sort of neighbours and friends I would meet. When would I catch up with my relatives? And how would I cope with speaking English?

6
Further Growth

Joining Stanley in London was not only the start of a new married life for me, but it was also a great adventure, to experience what I had read about London in books or heard about from friends. In these accounts, it all seemed perfect and rosy! I realised from our letters and phone calls that there was going to be lots for me to learn and to take in. I knew that this new life was going to be full of challenges for both of us, and that we would need God's guidance and immense wisdom. Along with this we also needed to get to know each other's habits and personalities, and we would need to work hard to make ends meet and to be able to afford to buy a house of our own, from where we could start a family.

Stanley had previously lived in Rochdale, a town in Greater Manchester, but he moved to London about a year before I arrived, following close friends who had made the same move to London shortly before. They were like elder brothers to him. Stanley got a job in Wembley as a production controller. Along with this job, he started working in a driving school, where his interest grew in becoming a driving instructor himself, and later on he registered his own driving school.

The day I landed at Heathrow Airport it was a pleasant spring day. Stanley came to collect me with a friend and his small daughter. We arrived at their place to meet his wife, had breakfast and then we were dropped off at our rented flat in Earl's Court.

The next evening, Stanley drove me around the city, which I found fascinating. I could not believe that the dream I had in my schooldays about wishing to visit London at some time in my life was now becoming a reality. After such a long wait, it was exciting to realise that I was actually in London, not just for a visit but to live, and to make my home here.

It was also nice to meet and come to know some of Stanley's Pakistani friends and his cousin's family. I thought that in London everyone would be 'white British', but it was not quite so, as even back then London was home to many nationalities.

I soon learned about the frequent rain and the changing weather, that we could have four different seasons all in one day! I came with an open mind and tried to observe and absorb all the new experiences and situations, people's views and attitudes. Most shocking to me was that many people questioned the existence of God. I thought to myself, 'What sort of question is that, and is that a real concern in the UK?'

Gradually I learned that it is a free country, and everyone is entitled to their opinion, whereas my perception, coming from a Muslim country, was entirely different. In Pakistan, God's existence is never questioned, and for Christians He is their personal God and there is no doubt about it in their minds. People can be nominal Christians, but God is still central to their beliefs. My perception was that the UK was a Christian country and that there would not be any religious tensions, as everyone would adhere to and celebrate the Christian festivals, especially Christmas, but obviously this was not so – it has become a good excuse to receive presents, but is not a particularly religious occasion for most!

It was pleasing to discover, however, that London was not as dusty as Pakistan can be, with its dry climate and high winds that blow the dust all around. Here in the UK we could get away from daily dusting and hoovering! The cleanliness and orderly way of life was quite impressive. I found that people were very punctual and had a great sense of responsibility. It was also very new for me to see that, unlike in Pakistan, women were able to work doing all kinds of jobs.

One of my relatives who worked in the British Embassy in Islamabad had mentioned to me that in Pakistan we suffer with religious persecution, whereas in Britain I would be more likely to suffer from racism. The issue of racism was new to me. I am happy to say that I did not experience any form of racism in my first job, in a contact lens company, as every department had an Asian person working there. I was not aware of any racism at the church level either, and I assumed that the UK was a Christian country and so Christians should be free of any hatred of this kind. Within myself I knew that all people were equal in the sight of God. All I felt that I needed to do at this time was to build my confidence in who I was and how to fit into this new society where I found myself. After all, I was a legal citizen here and had been given British nationality, and so could contribute fully to the society.

In general, I found that the culture was quite organised. One had a work routine for five days, the weekend off to catch up on housework, to rest and to relax. Yearly holidays were budgeted for and planned in advance. I felt this was the key to a good, contented, healthy life in a successful country. People seemed to be mostly honest, responsible and hard-working. Everyone was rewarded for their work and none of their wages were held back, as far as I knew. It was good to know that the less privileged, the unemployed, children, elderly and refugees were all looked after, and the basic state education and healthcare were free to all. It felt like that the laws were generally based upon the commandments of God. I knew that I needed to learn so much about life in the UK.

The time was coming for me to find a job, so Stanley took me by bus one evening to find a local job centre. The next morning, he gave me an *A to Z* map of London and marked the location of the job centre on it, so that I could find my way there on my own! I dutifully obeyed and on that first visit I was offered a job as a lab assistant in a contact lens company, which I accepted. I went straight to the company that day to register and was given a date to start working – the very next day. There, a senior member of staff gave me a tour of the workplace.

This was a good opportunity for me to learn about the working conditions in London and to know more about British culture. While working there I learned about baking cakes from a senior colleague, and about flower arranging when a Japanese member of staff held classes after work. I remember tasting my first pizza while at work, a vegetarian pizza brought in for me by an Indian colleague. It was not to my taste!

I opened my first bank account with some leftover lunch vouchers from work. It was a good discipline, helping me learn to organise my finances. It was helpful to have some Indian colleagues who could help me to understand things and to guide me, but still I had to think carefully before saying a sentence. I always recited Psalm 23 before leaving home, and received great comfort and assurance in knowing that 'the LORD is my shepherd', no matter what may come my way that day.

My primary need was to get into the habit of speaking the English language. Although I studied English literature as a subject from high school to degree level, we were not encouraged to actually speak in English. So, to aid with deepening my knowledge of the language, I joined a short evening course, which was a great help for my confidence. While there I met many students who had similar struggles with the English language, which reassured me that I was not alone in this problem.

My work was within walking distance from our flat, which was quite convenient. The English evening class was a one-stop train journey for me on the London Underground, which was another new experience for me, especially having trains that arrived mostly on time!

Once I left my handbag on the train, so I went to the London Underground lost property office, which was full of umbrellas! My handbag was there and although a small amount of money was missing, I was still impressed with the organised system of handling lost property.

Stanley always encouraged me in my work and language studies. He has always had a broad vision of things, making it clear that it is good for me to have a career and build my independence, as life is unpredictable and he might not always be around to help me. This made a lot of sense.

My habit of evening Bible reading continued for a while after my arrival in the UK, but then it started fading away as I got busy with the daily routine of work and language study. We did not join a local church but found a Hindi/Urdu Methodist fellowship in Southall King's Hall, though we only attended on special occasions. On our wedding anniversary on 31st December, after an evening out, Stanley always made an effort to find a nearby New Year's Eve midnight service to attend. It was always a struggle to find one when we were on the outskirts of London.

God – being faithful as always and true to His promises – did not leave me alone but continued to work His purpose out in my life, gradually and gently giving me time to settle well. During this period, I started having a recurring dream a few times a year. In the dream I had an exam the following day and could not find the right books to study, and began to panic. I had this dream from around 1975 to 1983. I did not know the meaning or the purpose behind it, whether it was of any significance or not. Was it a spiritual issue that needed the advice of a priest or other spiritual leader? Was God nudging me to get my attention? I only mentioned it to one or two people, but they felt that it was simply a result of the anxiety and stress that I had felt during the time of preparing for my degree exams, which had left an imprint on my mind, and that's what I was re-experiencing in my dream. So, I did nothing further about it at that time. I will talk more about this dream later.

After six months we moved from Earl's Court to Greenford in order to be closer to Stanley's workplace and also to find comparatively cheaper accommodation, so that we might save up for a place of our own. This meant that I had to commute back to Earl's Court for work. I used this time on the train to read from a small pocket-sized Urdu language New Testament that I had been given by a Muslim friend! This practice continued for a number of years until 1980. As a result, the journey was made more pleasurable and profitable for me, because I received comfort and spiritual nourishment.

My uncle in Surrey was in the car business and recommended a car for us to buy, a second-hand Ford Escort costing £250, which seemed like a lot of money to me, as we were saving up for a deposit on a house. However, it was a good investment that made life more convenient, especially when needing to travel in the rain or snow. This first car of ours was broken into and my Urdu language Bible was stolen (not the New Testament given to me by my Muslim friend), which I was sad about, given that it was my wedding gift from my dear aunt, my mother's sister. On the other hand, I hoped that it had gone to someone who needed it more than I did! On another occasion this same car was stolen, but fortunately it was found abandoned by the police, at the side of a main road. We breathed a great sigh of relief and were very appreciative of having such a conscientious police force.

Whenever we were in need of advice or help, we always had relatives who were there for us. We were treated like their own children. Over the years, we have built an ongoing, strong relationship with them. We were also blessed in having other relatives from Pakistan visit us during our early years of marriage. One of my uncles visited us in London on his journey back from Mexico to Pakistan, after attending a conference there. His sudden visit was a pleasant surprise for us. It was so good to meet a family member from back home after such a long time away from Pakistan. A few months later, my aunt, my father's youngest sister, and her family arrived from Libya to attend a relative's wedding. They stayed with us over the Christmas season and celebrated all the festive activities with us. It was a great joy for me to be able to meet up with my cousins for the first time in many years.

Stanley had the weekends off and, apart from doing the weekly shop, he had time on his hands. I suggested that he could make use of his driving instructor's licence to work part-time at the weekends. So he started working in a local driving school for extra income, in order that we could obtain a mortgage, though we still needed to borrow some money from our bank for a deposit.

We were able to buy a house of our own in Alperton, which we moved into in August 1977.

When our daughter was born, in November 1977, we decided to name her Rebecca, as Stanley's mother had said about me, 'I have found Rebecca for my son Isaac.'[3]

Rebecca was the first grandchild in both of our families. She was a special gift of God to us. She was a very calm, quiet and contented child. As she was growing up alone at that point – our son was born in 1983 – she got used to entertaining herself. When Rebecca was three months old,

---

[3] See Genesis 24.

I went back to work as we needed the extra income to pay for the refurbishments required for our new home, leaving Rebecca with a local childminder. Again, God's gracious hand was upon us, guiding and leading us to accomplish the plans that He had for us.

Stanley suggested that I go to Pakistan for a lengthy period before Rebecca started school. I saw the sense in this, as I would not have this opportunity again in the future. Rebecca and I stayed for five months. Stanley joined us for part of the time, although he had to return earlier for work. I enjoyed being with my family and friends, taking the opportunity to rest and relax. At this point, Rebecca was three years old.

I felt like a stranger back in Pakistan, for it was changing so fast. There was lots of new technology, everyone wanted to own a VCR to watch videos at home. Capitalism was on the rise from 1975 onwards but contentment was in decline! One positive, however, was that after experiencing the fast pace of life in London, where people run to catch the bus and train for fear of being late for work, in contrast life was much more relaxed and laid back for people in Pakistan. Leaving things until tomorrow has never been a problem for them.

Before leaving for Pakistan, I had resigned from my job at the contact lens company. So I returned to England not really knowing what my life would look like.

7
Pruning Time

Back in the UK, I stayed at home so that I could take Rebecca to and from a local nursery school. During this time, I worked from home, managing the administration for the driving school that Stanley had started in 1977.

We had all the basic necessities of life at our home in Alperton, Wembley. Hospitality and openness to welcome visitors and relatives from Pakistan was very much part of our family life. Alperton itself has changed a lot in recent years. Most of the shops were English-owned, but Alperton was starting to change, as Indians from Kenya were settling into the area. Alperton was becoming a centre of attraction, with Indian gold and sari shops and large grocery markets, just like in Southall. It was gradually becoming a predominantly Indian shopping area. Prior to that, there had been only one English grocery shop at the bottom of the Ealing Road, where I queued to be served. In contrast to recent years, I did not have the option of different pack sizes or varieties; I just had to buy whatever was there. Soon after that, rows of large ethnic supermarkets appeared along the road, where many of the spices and vegetables from around the world were available to buy.

I started to learn to drive with Stanley as my instructor. But when it came to reversing round a corner, Stanley lost his patience with me and began to raise his voice. At this point I stopped the car, got out of the driving seat and refused to carry on! Stanley had to drive me back home.

I restarted lessons when Rebecca was a little older, but this time not with Stanley. Instead, a colleague from the contact lens company, who also was a trainee driving instructor, taught me. I passed my test at the first attempt in 1980. This was the year in which all three of us visited Pakistan, as mentioned earlier, and we were able to celebrate Rebecca's third birthday with our extended family. This was our first time back there since I had left for the UK five years previously. My sister got married while we were there, so it was a privilege for us to meet the rest of her new family as well.

When Rebecca was four years old, she was accepted full-time into our local school nursery. Stanley's wish was to educate her in a private school, but I was quite concerned about how he would manage to bear all the expenses while I was not working – and what would happen if we had more children? Would we be able to do the same for them? Still, with God's grace he managed somehow, and to that end he started working long hours in order to manage the mortgage and the other expenses on his own, Rebecca transferring to a private school for girls the following year.

Rebecca was christened at a Methodist church where we often worshipped. Then, somehow, we came to know about a Pakistani fellowship that met in St Mary's Church,

Islington. It had been started as a home group by three brothers. God blessed their faithfulness and persistence, and from 1969 this home group became a fellowship under the leadership of Rev Daniel Singh. It was the very first Pakistani fellowship within the Church of England, so we went to explore it. It was about seven miles away from Alperton. There we met a Pakistani priest. He was sitting alone in the chapel, waiting for people to turn up to pray with him before the four o'clock service. He was glad to meet us and we had a short worship time there with him. We made it a regular habit to join him every Sunday, and as numbers grew, the decision was made to move into the main church worship area.

Attending St Mary's Church was a great blessing for us, especially as we got to know many Pakistani Christians and built up good friendships. At Christmas, Easter and on other special occasions many commuted from all over London, coming to worship together in their native Urdu language. For me, reading the Bible in Urdu and singing psalms and hymns in Punjabi and Urdu meant a lot, as it was the language of my heart, as it also must have been for all the first generation of immigrants. In my very early years in London, I had been to another church, where my uncles worshipped, but singing English hymns seemed very foreign to me as I was unfamiliar with their tunes. But I noticed the richness of their theology as I hummed along with the music.

While members of St Mary's Church, we were invited to two of the very first wedding ceremonies to take place from within the Pakistani fellowship there and to two christenings. These were opportunities for us to meet more Pakistani families from all over London.

A few years later, the fellowship was offered a large, closed church building in the Tufnell Park area that could be used by the Pakistani fellowship to be their new home. Church members repaired and painted the old church building so that it was fit for regular use again. The old-fashioned heating system was not in very good condition, however, so Stanley's job each Sunday was to just keep it going! It was a very large church with a high ceiling and could get very cold. So in wintertime it was decided that we should meet in the chapel area for worship. The Sunday school was run by a member and one of her English friends, both commuting from Kent each Sunday.

Rebecca was confirmed at the age of thirteen in this church, All Saints, Tufnell Park, along with a few other young people, by the local bishop of our area at that time. That was a joyous and important occasion for the fellowship. I got involved in the reading rota and later began to manage the church accounts as well. Our vicar was not paid any stipend from the fellowship. He was only paid £50 for his travel expenses, and because of that he always struggled to make ends meet. Because of this, the church committee decided to give him a small salary of £250 a month, once our giving as a congregation had become more stable. His committed service kept the fellowship going over many years, until his health started to deteriorate.

A freelance evangelist and his family joined the fellowship, arriving from Libya on a work visa. From time to time, the evangelist was given the opportunity to preach, and we joined his home group. The Bible study and prayer time gave us renewed depth of insight into the Scriptures. His passion for the gospel and love for the Lord brought a breath of fresh air to the fellowship and to the whole Christian Pakistani community around London.

Looking back now, I believe God was using all of this in my life, preparing me for some future role, just as He did with His kings and prophets before calling them to His service. He trained and corrected them according to what was necessary for their individual growth, sometimes taking many years before they were ready to embark upon their callings.

Our second child, Sharoon (Rocky), was born in 1983. This year had been a very challenging time for us. It seemed as if the foundations of our marriage were being shaken by a severe storm. For me, it was a time of deep thinking, remorse and lots of unanswered questions. Our family life had been disrupted as Stanley was out a lot, busy working hard to make ends meet, so we were not seeing much of him. But God is good; He can bring good out of any situation. As it says in Romans 8:28, 'And we know that in all things God works for the good of those who love him, who have been called according to his purpose.' God was true in His faithful promise made to me back in Pakistan, that our house would be built on the Rock.

In 1986, my father visited us in London for a few months. He would regularly accompany us to this Pakistani fellowship. One Sunday, he was even given the opportunity to preach in the service. He was also a good handyman; he helped us around the house and with the launderette business, which we had bought in 1982. These months spent together as a family were a wonderful time. Also, quality time spent with his grandchildren was valuable.

The unrest was increasing in my soul and mind, perhaps because of a distant relationship with God. Maybe a deep intimacy was needed and my soul was thirsty for it. But God was closer than I would have imagined and revealed His promise of forgiveness. One morning while I was in the garden, spreading Rocky's clothes on the washing line, a thought like a flash crossed my mind: 'If I repent, the blood of Jesus once shed on the cross can forgive and cleanse me from all unrighteousness.'[4] This was an awesome revelation of God's love to me that I could act upon and be forgiven.

The time and the day came. While Stanley, Rocky and Rebecca were sleeping, I sat on my bed and poured out my heart to God with tears, pleading for forgiveness for not really being committed to Him. God heard the cry of my heart and within a few minutes I felt the unbelievable, awesome presence of God in my soul. It made me feel so light and peaceful as my prayer had been answered and I knew I had been cleansed and forgiven. It seems hard to explain, as words are not enough. It was like chains had fallen off and I had been set free! I felt a great assurance of the reality of Jesus dying for my sins.

The presence was so real and awesome and I wanted to stay in it. At that point I prayed, 'Lord, no matter what life throws at me, or whatever the future holds for me, or when I go through hard times, please don't ever take Your presence away from me.' Although this experience was a one-off, it was very real, unforgettable, very peaceful and full of the assurance of forgiveness. I became more aware

---

[4] See 1 John 1:9.

of the free gift of the Holy Spirit and continued to practise differentiating His voice from my own thinking.

I was so sure of my personal encounter with the living Christ and of His forgiveness. Stanley and I both felt that this was a wake-up call for us, that we had been taking God's good gifts for granted, and we proposed to make a concerted effort to spend more time together as a family in the future.

From that point onwards, I would kneel beside my bed for a long time each night giving thanks to God and praying. I am not able to recall the exact content of my prayers; all I knew was that the Holy Spirit was prompting me to pray. This whole experience of repentance and forgiveness became central to my faith in Christ. My eyes were opened afresh to the things of God. For example, when I had passed church buildings in the past, they had meant little to me, but now I saw the possibilities of God moving in those areas and felt great joy and expectancy, that God was indeed at work.

Later, I shared this experience with the minister from the Methodist church I'd been attending. He explained to me that I had encountered new life in Christ, and he rejoiced with me in the grace of God.

After this period of repentance, the Libyan evangelist made a visit to our house and asked if I read the Bible as well as praying. I said, 'I hear the Word from your sermons, isn't that enough?' He replied, 'Just praying and not reading the Bible is like just drinking water and not having solid food.' I thought about this and realised that there was a void in my life which was as yet unfulfilled. I took his words quite seriously and knew that my Bible reading had tailed off. I knew I had to start to read it in earnest and with full commitment. The hunger and zeal were growing in me. For me, the difficult question was where to restart reading, as the Bible is a big book! Where should I begin, the Old Testament or the New Testament?

One evening I felt it was the moment to begin! I sat alone with my Urdu Bible (my aunt had kindly replaced the one that had been stolen) in the front room and began to read from the Gospel of Matthew. Then I woke up quite early in the morning, turned on the bedside lamp and carried on reading. I was on the third chapter of the Gospel of Matthew – it is about John the Baptist, preaching, 'Repent, for the kingdom of heaven has come near' (v2). Suddenly my eyes were opened and I understood that the Bible was the subject I had not prepared for – this was the meaning of the dream I had been having for the past seven or more years, ever since I had arrived in England!

I found much about dreams from God in the Scriptures. In Daniel 2:29, our God is described as 'the revealer of mysteries'. I was amazed and overjoyed, seeing God's sovereignty and guiding hand at work in my life. I was overwhelmed with how patient and caring God truly is and how He can be so interested in the individual. From that point on, God's deep love began to be impressed upon me. As it says in John 3:16-17:

> For God so loved the world that he gave his one and only Son, that whoever believes in him shall not perish but have eternal life. For God did not send his Son into the world to condemn the world, but to save the world through him.

In the mystery dream, I was always struggling to prepare for an exam the next day. I didn't have enough time and I could not work out the name of the subject that I needed to prepare for. I had a heap of books in front of me, covering many different subjects and I went through all of them, but still could not find the correct book! Each time the anxiety of this mystery dream would wake me up and I would think to myself, 'I have already taken and passed all these exams, so what is this repeated dream all about?' Now I realised what the missing book was, the subject I was not prepared for – it was the Bible! My heart leaped for joy with the real nature of God, who is so wise and organised and works so systematically.

It is said by some that if God cannot get your attention during the day, then He speaks to you in the night through dreams. Dreams are often very significant in the Bible, and it has been a common way for God to communicate with humans throughout the ages. In the Old Testament, we read in Genesis 28 that Jacob had a dream where he saw a stairway to heaven with angels 'ascending and descending on it' (v12). In Genesis 41, we see that God spoke to Pharaoh about the upcoming famine through two dreams. Joseph, Daniel and King Solomon were all spoken to by God through dreams. In the New Testament, in Matthew 1:20, God speaks to Joseph, Mary's husband, in a dream, instructing him to take Mary home as his wife. The wise men in Matthew 2:12, and Pontius Pilate's wife in Matthew 27:19, were spoken to through dreams.

In my case, the narrative of the dream was clear but the meaning was only revealed after I surrendered my way to His will. As I understood, He made me humble and taught me the meaning and depth of true repentance. I believe, among my many shortcomings, my weak personality needed to be strengthened. I needed to be able to take a stand in difficult circumstances.

I was amazed and felt so special. God had been so patient, waiting for me to turn to Him and to be able to understand the meaning of the dream. 'Where are You leading me, Lord,' I thought, 'with all this preparation?'

8
Feeding Time

After this encounter and experiencing God's peace and forgiveness, I started meditating more on who this God is, who loves me and who has saved me. As I started thinking on these matters, I started getting more and more confused. The question that I could not answer was, 'If this is God whom I met, then who is Jesus?' At that stage I did not discuss this with anyone. I may well have been thinking, 'This is not the right question to ask about my faith and it is not honouring God to ask such questions.' From childhood, faith was something that one accepted without asking any questions. Thinking critically about these matters was never encouraged. So I left it there, thinking it would resolve itself in due course, and indeed it did.

Over time, as I my understanding deepened, the doctrine of the Trinity became clearer and clearer to me, one God in three Persons. I understand the questions of those who don't agree or comprehend the biblical status of Jesus, being God in human form, the Lord and Saviour of the whole world.

I carried on praying and reading the Bible regularly. I decided to start reading from the beginning. When I reached the books of Kings and Chronicles, my enthusiasm waned, and I stopped reading through the rest of the Bible. I found the grace to read through the whole Bible much later, in 2018, and did so in almost three years. I must confess that I don't remember everything I read but the joy and the contentment was overwhelming. Another reason I wanted to read through the Bible was that I felt unfamiliar with the stories and names often shared by our Asian senior women who read the Bible and used to mention things, people and events from the Scriptures.

Prior to this I listened to the English version on CDs with the Bible open, but it was not like reading and meditating on the Word. I value reading both the Testaments to try to understand the text in the light of both its original context and its application for today.

It seems to me that reading the whole Bible is a very cultural thing – maybe that is owing to having been brought up in a country where the Quran is read through at special occasions in one seating by thirty or so people. My family would read the Bible regularly from beginning to end. And it is a blessing to learn passages of Scripture by heart. This habit of reading through the Bible is built into Christians from Pakistan (and maybe other countries too) right from childhood; learning parts of the Scriptures, especially from the Psalms, is also encouraged in Sunday schools.

As the time passed, I began to feel spiritually low and empty. I did not know what I was going through until one day there was a knock on the front door. There before me were two Jehovah's Witnesses and, in my naivety, wanting to learn more about the Bible, I invited them in. They came back a few times until the subjects of the divinity of Christ and of the Holy Spirit came up in our conversations. I was bold enough to confess my faith before them, that I was a Christian, and shared my experience of meeting the living Christ through His Holy Spirit. I never saw them again!

The experience helped me to reflect on what I knew to be true about Jesus and His Holy Spirit, who filled my life. Since then, I have come to understand about spiritual emptiness, and that I need to 'refuel' myself through fellowship with other believers, to be encouraged and to learn more.

I knew that Jesus Christ is man, but also God, and that the Holy Spirit is God too, both being one with the Father. The Bible says, 'But when the set time had fully come, God sent his Son, born of a woman, born under the law, to redeem those under the law, that we might receive adoption to sonship' (Galatians 4:4-5). To the unbelieving Jews who wanted to hear from Jesus Himself whether or not He was the Christ, the Messiah, He said, 'I and the Father are one' (John 10:30). Jesus also spoke about the Holy Spirit, saying, 'The Advocate, the Holy Spirit, whom the Father will send in my name, will teach you all things and will remind you of everything I have said to you' (John 14:26).

The Bible witnesses that Jesus is God in the flesh – see for example John 1:1, Colossians 2:9 and Hebrews 1:3. I appreciate that this can be difficult to grasp. For example, on one occasion my seven-year-old granddaughter came to me and asked, 'I am a bit confused, there is God and there is Jesus, how come there are two?'

I replied, 'There is the Holy Spirit as well, but we do not say there are three Gods. We believe in one God with three characters, who have different roles but who work together in unity.' She listened very carefully, and we hope and pray that one day she will come to a fuller understanding of her faith. And I'm sure she will have even more questions by then!

Stanley observed me praying and reading my Bible more frequently and so asked me, 'What sort of career would you like to pursue?'

My answer was, 'I would like to serve the Lord.'

He replied, 'You need to be properly trained, then. You cannot just pick up the Bible and go around preaching.'

Later on, I asked our vicar about this possibility. He told me, 'Training for ministry will be quite hard for you. It is not easy to train for ministry.' Maybe from his own experience, being an immigrant to the country and English not being his first language, he recognised the difficulties involved, so I left it there for the time being.

Within that same year, our vicar started having heart problems. His health deteriorated rapidly and in one of the services he said that his wish was that someone from within the congregation would lead us forward. Two men raised their hands in response to this – one was a member of our congregation and the other was a visitor from Libya (not the evangelist mentioned earlier).

I was sitting at the back with our son, Rocky, who was about a year and a half old by then, and he was asleep in my lap. Hearing the vicar's desire, a small voice within me said, 'Should I offer myself for this ministry?' I spoke back to myself, 'This cannot be for me, because of my academic and English language limitations.' Once again, I left it and forgot all about it.

Then one day we heard the shocking and sad news that our vicar had died from a massive heart attack. All the families from church took it in turn to visit his wife and family to offer their condolences. According to our tradition, we brought food with us so that the family didn't have to worry about cooking and would have time to grieve and to prepare for the funeral. Enough food is brought on these occasions to share with all in attendance. Also, when elders or pastors visit, Scriptures are read and prayers are said with the family.

The vicar's funeral was conducted by the Archdeacon of Hackney. During the memorial service, our local bishop shared our vicar's wish that someone from this congregation should be trained to carry on his duties. By that time, I had forgotten about the small voice suggesting I lead the congregation. So I didn't say anything. In fact, no one said anything. Then, to my surprise, I heard the voice of my husband, Stanley – sitting way ahead of me – saying, 'What about my wife?'

'What about your wife?' the bishop replied. 'She will need to come to see me!' His meaning was that we could then discuss the possibility further. This seemed as though it could be the beginning of my journey into the ministry!

I would like to honour God for His provision here. Even before I entered the selection process, He provided the finances that we would need in order for me to train for the ministry. Stanley worked hard to provide for all of us. I believe God has blessed me greatly by giving me Stanley as my husband to support me in my ministry in many ways.

When I went to meet the area bishop, I did not know what to say in order to justify my desire to serve in this capacity. All I could do was to share my life story from childhood and my experience of personal repentance and meeting with the living God through His Holy Spirit. The bishop made me a cup of tea and, as I was getting a bit tearful, he handed me a box of tissues. This conversation was to be the first part of my interview process.

I also had further interviews with the bishop. It seemed to me as if he did not know exactly what to do with me! Since he wanted to find out about women's ministry in Pakistan, he invited some missionaries, who had connections with Pakistan and who had worked there, to attend on one such occasion. Their experience was that currently women were not involved directly in church ministry, though they could work as 'Bible Women', who would visit housewives in their homes for Bible study and prayer.

Eventually I was recommended for non-stipendiary ministry (NSM), meaning that I would work for approximately twenty hours a week, not getting paid a salary but being able to claim expenses. For this I had to attend part-time training at Oak Hill Theological College in Southgate, London. When I phoned Oak Hill to confirm my place there, the voice on the other end of the line gave me a foretaste of the place. The voice was that of one of the tutors, and it was soft, kind and gentle. Later on, during my time there I went and thanked her for this initial experience of college life!

Stanley provided a car for me and bore all the expenses for my books, while the bishop wrote to various Asian

Christian organisations in order to acquire financial support to cover my tuition fees.

I started college in September 1987. I would attend every Tuesday evening for two hours. This was also where I first experienced eating English food, as we were served supper before the lecture began, with many people coming straight from work. Once a year, before the summer break, we had a summer school to learn about a particular subject in detail; we also had periodic residential weekends. I remember one such occasion, sitting alone in the college dining room, gazing out of the window at the lovely green grounds outside, when I had a strong sense of God confirming to me that this was the reason He had brought me to England, to be at Oak Hill College to be trained for His ministry.

I have been asked many times what made me start covering my head when leading church services. The truth of the matter is that it was at Oak Hill that I first did this. One evening, two of us had been asked to lead the evening prayers and beforehand we prayed together in the side room. Unconsciously, I covered my head with a traditional scarf called a *dupatta*, part of the traditional Pakistani dress. My colleague commented that it was a nice gesture of humbling oneself for prayers. I took this as a sign of encouragement and acceptance of my heritage. From that point onwards, I have continued with this practice of covering my head whenever I pray or lead a service.

I had no fear of engaging with the theological studies at Oak Hill, despite realising how hard I might find them. One growing concern I did have, though, was how I would choose the two connected readings required when preaching, one from the Old Testament, one from the New. It was not until later that I realised that the Lectionary is available, with readings already set out according to the Christian calendar for the whole year!

While training we were set thirty essays which we had to complete within the three years. At this time, I could barely type in English so it was a steep learning curve for me! Stanley even tried to find people who could type for me, with me writing the essays by hand in advance. On top of all this, at that time I had never read the Bible in English before and did not even know the names of the books in English. For this reason, I had no hesitancy in taking my Urdu Bible along with me to the lectures, as well as the English version, so that I could understand the topics better. There were so many different 'ologies' to be learned and understood! It was like starting primary school all over again.

I was the only woman of Pakistani origin in the whole college, but I never felt like an outsider or different from the other students, as everyone was so considerate and understanding towards me, and happy to help and guide me. Most of my colleagues were professionals or had retired from their jobs and were now called to serve in this way. Maybe I was the only one there who was a housewife with no such profession or relevant qualifications. I felt that studying at this higher level would have been easier for me if I had been educated here in Britain, as in my teenage years, Pakistani standards of education in state schools were not as high as those in British ones. When I shared my concerns with one of my colleagues, that I was just a housewife, straightaway she encouraged me.

Having said all of this, I know that God is Almighty, and He calls and chooses whoever He wants, for His glory, to serve His purposes in many different ways. All I needed was to surrender my will to His mighty will, in obedience and with a humble attitude. And He would take care of the rest in accordance with His promises.

When Jesus was giving the final instructions to His disciples about giving the good news of the kingdom of God to all the nations, He said:

> All authority in heaven and on earth has been given to me. Therefore go and make disciples of all nations, baptising them in the name of the Father and of the Son and of the Holy Spirit, and teaching them to obey everything I have commanded you. And surely I am with you always, to the very end of the age.
> (Matthew 28:18-20)

Also in Philippians 4:6-7 it states,:

> Do not be anxious about anything, but in every situation, by prayer and petition, with thanksgiving, present your requests to God. And the peace of God, which transcends all understanding, will guard your hearts and your minds in Christ Jesus.

The following verses from Isaiah became a source of great assurance to me:

> But now, this is what the LORD says –
> he who created you, Jacob,

he who formed you, Israel:
'Do not fear, for I have redeemed you;
I have summoned you by name; you are mine.'
(Isaiah 43:1)

For me, studying at Oak Hill was the biggest challenge of my life. I suffered with lots of stress and anxiety, trying to complete my assignments on time. In the first year, I began to suffer with vitiligo, a condition causing discolouration in patches of the skin, owing to lack of pigmentation. This condition has not attracted much research and there is little treatment for it, but one of the causes could be anxiety and stress.

In the beginning, I was quite self-conscious about it, and my question was, 'Why this, Lord, at the time when I am preparing to study?' Still, God never let me down and His mighty provision kept me moving forward. One of the General Practitioners from my surgery did refer me to Hammersmith Hospital, where I was given a few minutes of radiation each week. This, however, made no difference at all, and I was subsequently recommended to obtain a camouflage cream from an NHS beautician, who combined two different shades of the cream to match the colour of my skin, in order to cover the patches.

The patches themselves came and went, but I was not anxious about them any more. I knew that God was in control of the entire situation; I believed that God does not give us more than we can bear, but that He also provides a way out for us. As it says in the Bible, when talking about temptations, 'God is faithful; he will not let you be tempted beyond what you can bear. But when you are tempted, he will also provide a way out so that you can endure it' (1 Corinthians 10:13). It wasn't a 'temptation' as such, but I took these verses as a promise from God to encourage me in many of life's difficult situations, bringing assurance and future hope.

Also, God could use my struggles to bless others – an example of this being when one of my fellow students who struggled with their own academic work told me that I was brave to carry on with my studies despite having limited English, and that they found encouragement from my example!

In the final year of my studies, we were required to go on a church placement, and St James Church, Alperton, was chosen for me by one of my tutors. As soon as the vicar received my referral letter, he, along with his wife, came to meet me. They were surprised that they had not heard about my family living in the parish before. Though I had lived in Alperton for fourteen years at this point, I also had never heard of St James Church, though there were five families on my street who attended!

During my placement, the church was meeting in the church hall, situated on the main Ealing Road, as a new building was under construction. In the year following my placement, I was invited back to preach at St James Church on St James' Day and again, to share my experience of motherhood on Mothering Sunday. Similarly, the vicar was invited to preach to our Pakistani congregation at All Saints Church.

I waited to see where this was all heading, though I was at peace with it all.

9
Flowering

In 1990, after completing the three years of my NSM at Oak Hill Theological College, I was ordained deacon on St Andrew's Day at St Andrew's Church, Holborn, with a male member who was ordained as priest alongside my diaconate ordination. He had been partly trained in Pakistan, and was being priested to celebrated Holy Communion, while I, being ordained as a deacon, could not. Then I was licensed to work in All Saints Church, Tufnell Park. The service was attended by most of the Pakistani congregations from within the London area, and some of my colleagues and tutors from Oak Hill College attended as well.

Both of us were ordained by the Bishop of Stepney. The sermon was enriching, encouraging and thought-provoking. The whole service was a joyous occasion. After the service, we served homemade Pakistani food in the back of the church. It was the traditional biryani rice and roast chicken, both of which were enjoyed by all those present.

I chose the colour white for my *dupatta* so that it matched well with the dog collar. When I asked one of my tutors at Oak Hill what colour dresses I could wear, he said any colour but purple, as this colour was set aside for bishops only! Serving the Pakistani church, I was sure that I would not be told off for covering my head; in fact, quite the opposite might be true. In recent years the trend of wearing the *dupatta* is fading away among the younger generation. Only a few of us from the first generation of immigrants are keeping to this older tradition. Back in Pakistan, fashion is becoming more and more influenced by the West, though still within the constraints of modesty and cultural expectations.

After my ordination, I served for one year alongside the priest at All Saints Church, Tufnell Park. I sensed that my being a woman was an issue for some of my fellow Pakistani Christians. I also felt that I was not growing there. The church was some seven miles away from Alperton and so commuting there more than just once a week was not possible. Therefore, I could not really get involved in the local community or arrange midweek activities. Most of the church congregation were also commuting from distant areas and therefore we were having little impact on the local parish.

I shared my concern with our bishop. The bishop was retiring soon and wanted to see me settled somewhere permanent, so he suggested that I move back to St James Church, in our local parish, where I had completed my placement. I was happy to accept this new assignment, which clearly pleased the bishop as he raised his hands in the air and praised God, saying, 'I am sending you to a church with full life, where you can flower.'

I was licensed as a deacon in St James Church by the Archdeacon of Northolt on 2nd February 1992. The licence was the official permission to serve in St James'. I was thirty-nine years old. I wore a tailor-made Punjabi dress, designed for use with a dog collar. It was sewn for me by a neighbourhood friend. The service was attended by my previous Pakistani church members, close relatives and lots of St James Church members. A beautiful, large homemade fruit cake was cut to mark the occasion, made by a very gifted church member. A traditional Pakistani lamb biryani was served for lunch. Over the years, whenever I made basmati rice, people would say, 'Oh, it's Amelia's rice!' This was always a pleasant gesture of encouragement to me.

At St James', I was warmly welcomed and accepted by all, with no one seeming to have a problem with me being a woman! One or two people did ask my views about women's ordination and were satisfied with my explanation – that I felt that God had called me to serve in this way. To me, it was like we were being adopted into a loving, godly family. Stanley and I were particularly pleased that our children would learn about God in the language they were now most familiar with – English!

In St James Church I had the privilege to serve in all four services, including the midweek one. It was an honour to serve in a brand-new church building, St James Church Centre, which had been opened on 23rd June 1990. It had two large folding partitions downstairs, allowing the worship area to vary in size and creating two rear halls, one being used by a nursery school during the week. It also had a fully equipped kitchen and a side lounge used for meetings and prayer times before the services. There was a church office and a large hall upstairs that could be used for many different activities. This type of multipurpose church building was very new to me. It was ideal for helping to develop community relations through various projects such as a parent and toddlers' group, lunch clubs for the local school, and breakfast and after-school clubs.

I was accepted well by the wardens and church members alike. It was a great privilege to work with the vicar, the curate, who had also been trained at Oak Hill College, and the three readers. I learned a lot from their various experiences in ministry, their maturity in the faith, and also they helped me with my understanding of British culture and the church services. I noticed that St James' was mainly a white British church with some West Indian immigrants. My previous understanding was that all clergy come from Christian backgrounds and that the rest of their families would be committed Christians too. I soon learned that this was not always true, that here everyone was free to either believe in God or not.

My family and I were among the first Pakistanis to join St James Church. I settled in well, even getting used to leading services in the English language. The set services prescribed in the ASB (the Alternative Service Book) and BCP (Book of Common Prayer) were particularly challenging for me, as the service moved quickly from one page to another, sometimes missing out whole pages completely! It was also interesting learning how to add your own prayers to the given set prayers.

I found the vicar, John Root, to be a true Anglican and faithful servant. He started services on the dot and was sure to finish on time, so that the next service did not have to start late. He would make sure that everyone on the service rota was there in good time, in order to keep a sense of order and reverence within the service. His experienced management skills helped shape St James' into an organised and disciplined place of worship. He would handwrite the draft rotas for approval by all the church participants before finalising them and then writing a final version out again. He believed in holding lots of staff meetings to raise any new concerns for the church and to discuss new ways of helping the members to grow into strong and mature Christians. Scripture readings were chosen prayerfully for the next set of preaching rotas; either a book or a topic was chosen according to the needs of the congregation. I would meet with the vicar one-to-one every month to review my ministry up until the time I started working daily in the church after-school club.

Looking back now, I can see how limited my understanding of God was at that time. God has now become more real and alive to me, a God whom I can experience, not just someone to pray to in times of difficulty in order to get my needs met. I listen to His voice and obey, understanding that His ways are not always our ways.[5] I have learned a lot more of the truths found in the Bible and how to apply these truths in my daily life. Listening to the sermons and teaching of Rev John Root over the years has helped me a lot. I remember being taught about handling and managing money, as part of the series on giving, that if we manage and budget wisely then we don't need to do two jobs or lots of overtime, so we don't need to be 'too busy' to attend church regularly or to have time to rest and spend time with our families.

---

[5] See Isaiah 55:8.

Preparing sermons took me a lot of time and effort, yet I endeavoured to fulfil my assigned preaching slots as best I could. The vicar was happy to cover for me when necessary or to get the curate to help me out. In preparing for my sermons, I would try to read around the subject, looking at Bible commentaries and other reference books, which all helped me to grow in my biblical understanding. Initially I would write my sermons in pencil, which was easy to rub out and correct, before progressing to using a pen. Rebecca was a teenager by then, and was therefore able to proofread my sermon scripts for grammar and English mistakes. For my very first sermon, the vicar kindly listened while I read it through to him. I remember it was on the subject of the Good Shepherd. Stanley took time off work to be there for this. He would often give me feedback when I preached.

Learning how to type my sermons on a computer came much later for me, in around 2006. One of my cousins was staying with us while doing further studies, and with her encouragement I bought a laptop and began to learn how to use it, with her help. I was very pleased when I managed to type my first complete sermon on the laptop. I knew that this would help me greatly in my preparation and in delivering my sermons with confidence and clarity. I am still learning to expand my computer skills, as and when I need them. My children are often on hand to help when things get too complicated for me, as technology seems to be ever changing faster and faster!

One amusing incident happened just before I preached one Sunday morning. I placed my notes on the lectern, partially under the cloth for safekeeping. When I returned to check everything before the service, to my shock, my notes were missing! Where had they gone? I didn't have access to my computer to print them out again. I had no idea what to do! A thought came to my mind, and I ran to the office to check the bin. To my relief, there in the bin, all in one piece, were my sermon notes. I offered up a quick prayer of thanks to God!

Alongside my regular duties at the church, I was given the responsibility of running the parent and toddlers' group every Wednesday morning. For me, this was the beginning of getting to know my local community and their social needs. The parents that attended enjoyed making new friends there and exchanging their child-raising experiences with each other. I considered it a great privilege to be able to show God's love to the local community in this informal way. We were also able to invite these families to our summer festivals and carol services.

I learned the value of being involved in these kinds of groups – they helped to enrich my understanding of my local community. As I met the mothers of different backgrounds, I could often communicate in their native languages. Senior members of the church would also come along to chat with the mothers over a cup of tea, and then help pack away afterwards, which was a great help and support to me.

Two years into my service at St James', the big, debated issue of women's priesthood came to the forefront, after ten years of discussions. The year 1994 was the landmark for women Deacons to be priests for the first time in the history of the Church of England. I had been in ministry as a deacon for a total of three years by then, and was asked by our bishop if I would like to be put forward for priesthood ordination. I was given about six months to pray about it and to seek God's guidance on this issue. Personally, this was not an easy decision for me to take, as there was a large difference of opinion in the wider Church as to whether women should be priests, with some male clergy threatening to leave the Church of England if this went ahead.

I wanted to be fully sure within myself that this was the correct step for me to take, as I did not want to have any regrets over my decision afterwards. I consulted our Dean of Women, who gave me Bible passages to meditate on. She prayed with me and gave me some books to read, encouraging me to seek God's guidance in this matter. In the meantime, I went on holiday to Pakistan and left the issue totally in God's hands.

On my return, I met up with the bishop again in order to let him know my final decision. By this time, I felt sure that this was the correct step to take, so I had no hesitation in saying, 'Yes' to the bishop, who praised God at this news! This was my first personal experience of prolonged waiting on God, to know His will for sure, so as to not have any future regrets over my decisions.

The 16th April 1994, the day of my ordination, came. Seventy-four of us were divided into two groups and were ordained in two days. I was in the first group and it was quite a scary time for all the women being ordained, as we noted that there were people with banners outside St Paul's Cathedral protesting against this service. Later we came to know that there was an attempt to get a last-minute injunction to stop the service proceeding and the bishop had to wait for final clearance before he could commence.

Once robed, we were escorted into a side hall where the bishop was standing with a mobile phone in his hand, waiting for the go-ahead. If the answer was a 'No', then there was a plan to escort all the thirty-two women ordinands from London to Bristol Cathedral, so that the ordinations could still happen, as this was where the very first service of the ordination of women had already been held previously on 12th March 1994. For all of us, it seemed like a long wait for history to be made. We stayed still and calmly hoped for the best outcome. There was silence, our ears attentive to hear the phone ring. We waited patiently, holding our breath!

10
First Fruits

Then, suddenly, the phone rang. It seemed that the bishop was as nervous as we were! We could sense what the answer was, seeing the big smile appear on the bishop's face. It was positive! Straightaway we were instructed to be escorted into the cathedral. However, even then it was not all cut and dried.

Before the service itself actually started, a member of the clergy who opposed the ordination of women was given five minutes to speak his mind. With this finished, the service could finally proceed. Praise the Lord!

From that day onward, I, along with all the priestly women clergy, could celebrate Holy Communion in our churches. The very next day, I celebrated my first Holy Communion at St James Church. My close family and friends and many from the Christian Pakistani community attended the service, with Stanley organising for mutton biryani to be enjoyed by all those who attended.

Since the priesting of women signalled a great change within the Anglican Church, the local newspaper representative came to take photos and interviewed me, with the story appearing in the next issue.

Marking this historical day for the wider Church, all the national newspapers and television channels broadcast the news as their headline. This resolution was supposed to be applied to the rest of the worldwide Anglican Communion. It was a much discussed, debated and obviously much prayed about issue within the Church Communion as people tried to find God's clear guidance on this matter.

Having said this, the decision to ordain women as priests or not still remains a divisive issue within the individual church councils of specific provinces around the world. There is still much resistance to it in some countries. I can mention Pakistan here as an example, where women are still not allowed to be priested – they can be ordained deacons but are not permitted to celebrate the service of Holy Communion. To the best of my knowledge, they can lead prayers, do Bible readings, lead home groups, teach in seminaries and preach, and so on.

On the occasions when I return to Pakistan, I am still not recognised as a priest by the Anglican Church there, though I am welcomed by the free churches along with the Methodist and United Presbyterian.

My personal conviction about my ordination was that it was the fulfilment of my calling in the ministry of Jesus Christ. While serving as a deacon I felt that something was missing or as if there was a major difference between men and women. Now I am able to minister to others the love of God in Christ through the sacrament of the giving of bread and wine, His body and blood given once for all upon the cross, for my sins and those of the whole world. Every time I celebrate Communion, it is a humble and gracious reminder to me that I am standing where Jesus stood with His disciples at the Last Supper. When it comes to the point of absolution, my mind goes back to the reality and importance of my own experience of true repentance and the absolving of my sins by God Himself. So now, with confidence, I can offer this same forgiveness to all who turn to Jesus with true repentance.

Also now I was able to cover Communion services when the vicar was away on holiday, which was an added privilege for me, something which up until this time I had been unable to do.

My father was part of the ministry team in our family church in Faisalabad. In 1996, while leading a morning church service, he was taken ill. He suffered paralysis on his left side, which subsequently reduced his mobility considerably. After a few days in hospital, he was sent home to recover.

During this time, I had a dream in which I saw two coffins set side by side in a dimly lit room. I was unsure as to the meaning of the dream, and it left me slightly disturbed, especially as it contained two coffins! On the other hand, it did forewarn me of potential trouble ahead.

There is little in terms of a national health service in Pakistan, only expensive private alternatives. Therefore, my stepbrother and his wife took care of my father's daily long-term needs at home, with the help of my sister and her husband who lived nearby. A helper who lived in the neighbourhood was hired to assist with his care. My elder brother often visited with his family to be with him. I travelled over to Pakistan on my own and stayed there with my father for more than three months, while Stanley took care of the house and the children's schooling in the UK.

The family celebrated my father's seventy-second birthday along with friends, my siblings and his grandchildren. It was good that over these months I could get to spend some quality time with him. I helped with his medications and daily needs – it was my time to make up for all those years I had not seen him. It was a privilege for me to stay with him and help him out in this way.

While there, I had an opportunity to preach at my local family church. My father was sad that he was unable to come to hear me preach but was keen to give me some advice: 'Make sure your sermon is varied, with stories and illustrations to grab people's attention from the beginning, or else they may lose interest!'

I was much obliged to Rev John Root for allowing me to take this time off to go back to be with my father. On the day of my return, my father shed a tear, sad that I was leaving, and asked, 'Who is going to help me now?' I heard a sweet, small voice inside saying that I should return to visit in six months' time, but I did not say anything out loud as I did not want to make any promises that I might not be able to keep, so I kept this thought to myself, only sharing it with my sister. I regret that I did not obey the voice which said I should have to be there after six months, as it was exactly at this time that I heard the news of his death.

Sadly, the news of my father's death arrived exactly six months later. At the time I was getting ready to go to church for the midweek Communion service. When I arrived there, the vicar took me to the side and spent some time praying with me. The same day I carried on with my usual routine, hosting the home group lunch at my house. I didn't really have time to grieve, but later the thought of my father not being there hit me. Once alone, everything came out and I started to scream aloud. I subsequently felt a peace come upon me, reflecting on his strong Christian faith and that he was now with the Lord Jesus. Looking back, I realised that the dream I had had previously about the two coffins in the darkened room was all about my father's future. One coffin represented his severe, life-altering illness, the other his forthcoming death.

On the day of my father's funeral, he was washed and clothed at home and laid in the coffin. The funeral was then held on the same day in the courtyard of our house by the family vicar as the church was not within walking distance for everyone. Unfortunately, I was not able to attend owing to the short time gap between his death and burial. He was buried in the same graveyard as his father and mother. Most of the local families, our friends and his sisters and brothers were in attendance.

During my life, I had always dreaded the thought of losing him one day, as I did not know how I would be able to cope with such a great loss. However, I also knew that 'with God all things are possible' (Matthew 19:26) and that He would help me to bear this burden when the time came.

A few days after the funeral I dreamt that I saw my father standing in his usual white clothes, saying to me, 'I am all well now.' I took great comfort from this dream, knowing that at last he had been set free from all illness and disability, experiencing the ultimate healing that only God can bring.

Three years later, I once again returned to Pakistan for a visit to my stepmother. This time I was with Stanley and accompanied by both of our children. She was suffering with arthritis in her knees and so was struggling to walk. She did not look very well, but still always spent time in daily prayer. She always prayed for me and my family. Her simple faith and prayer life was an inspiration to me. She would often write to me, encouraging me and helping me to keep going, particularly during my early days in the UK when I was just settling in.

After returning from this trip to Pakistan and having been back in the UK for just ten days, we received the sad news of her death. Once again, there was little time for me to grieve.

For my stepmother's funeral, according to her wishes she was dressed in the white suit that I had previously given to her as a gift, and a garland of fresh flowers was put around her neck, just as it was at our grandmother's funeral. My sisters made sure that all of her last wishes were granted.

The chapter closed for my father and stepmother. But what was next for me, in the journey of faith? I was sensing the deeper need to enhance my education. I had not had a full-time secular job for many years. I felt 'unemployed' in a way, even with the obvious increase in my church responsibilities. Also, owing to the invention of the mobile phone, I was not needed as much by Stanley's company, as he could handle the bookings for his driving school from his car (obviously this was before the ban on the use of mobile phones while driving; and then of course we could use hands-free devices!).

After a few months of this, and with both children now at school, I felt a strong urge to find a church-based part-time job, which might aid me in gaining wider church experience. This was entirely my own decision, though Stanley supported me and had no objection.

During this time, I became aware of a vacancy at St James' after-school club, but I was told that the position had already been filled. I was unfortunately too late, but was told to pray for more children to join in the club, which would mean that they would then require another member of staff. I resolved to keep an eye out for future job vacancies at the club. I was sure that the job working with children in the church was for me, as it was part-time and could work very well with my ministry.

It was as if I was being led somehow towards this particular job. The summer break was approaching and I was asked to help out at the club during their summer scheme. This seemed a good opportunity to gain some preliminary experience. I was employed for just the four weeks of the summer scheme, as there was still no permanent position available. However, I felt strongly in my heart that eventually the job would be mine!

A few weeks into the term, a member of staff left, and the supervisor recommended that I should be given the job, so in September 1997 I was offered the role of play worker. After I had worked there for six months, I learned that the supervisor was planning to leave. The job was advertised locally for a few weeks, but I was not sure if I had enough experience for the role, so I did not apply. The Easter break was approaching and the desire was that the position would be filled before the start of the new term.

In the meantime, I attended a bishop's community ministry meeting in Ealing and on the way home, while driving along the Argyle Road, I heard an inner voice saying, 'Why don't you apply for the job?' I took this as a sign from God and was filled with positivity and joy. On returning home I phoned the chairperson of the after-school club management committee and asked whether the job was still available, and that if so, I would like to apply for it. He confirmed that it was still available, and so I applied. I went for an interview with Brent Council and was accepted on the basis that I would seek to complete further childcare training. I was also given paperwork to read on the subject of child protection and child abuse, as this was the time when this issue was starting to be taken more seriously and in need of being addressed at many different levels. I must admit that I was very ignorant of the widespread nature of the issue.

I started work as a supervisor after the Easter break in 1998. I went on to complete a basic training course in childcare, NVQ Level 2, which I did in 1999, and then NVQ Level 3 in 2004, along with other courses such as child protection, health and safety and food hygiene. Although I did not fully understand the reason or purpose behind God leading me towards this type of work, I still felt happy and content as I knew that I was in the right place and that I was growing and learning new skills within this role.

Looking back now, I can see that my spoken English was improving and my confidence was growing during this time of working with children. I am sure that it was God's way of training me for what lay ahead. I had the privilege of working alongside three more staff from the church and the community. The male staff member was always available to take the children outside to play football and to help during the summer schemes. He was also happy to help me with my typing! The staff were punctual and hard-working, all a great asset to the club. The children were happy and enjoyed the various activities on offer, especially the outdoor ones when the weather permitted.

Our summer schemes were great fun, including a coach trip and visits to local parks. I enjoyed the varied role, shopping for the daily snacks, completing timesheets, writing the staff wage cheques and arranging the daily activities. Stanley was happy to give me a hand each week in banking the club's fees. The club was thriving and we were getting close to full capacity. We were also getting new children coming to the club, whose mothers were being encouraged to attend training courses to increase their skill sets, and hence be able to go back into full-time work. Brent Council helped fund their childcare costs in order to facilitate this.

With our now substantial income, the club was able to repay the initial start-up loan of £5,000 to the church, which it had received two years previously. We were also now able to begin to pay rent to the church for the hire of the hall that we used. The club was regularly inspected by OFSTED and always given a good rating.

I would like to mention here one incident of theft that we had in the hall. One afternoon I noticed that the lock of the cupboard where the cash box was kept had been broken. I phoned the vicar to tell him about it. He came and prayed with me. I cannot recall the contents of the prayer, whether it was for us to find the money box or rather just for me to be at peace. When the vicar left, I sat alone, pondering the whole situation, wondering why it had to happen. Who could have done this and how did they get away unnoticed?

At this point a young man entered the hall and asked, 'Is this St James' after-school club?'

'Yes,' I replied.

'If you come with me,' he said, 'I can show you a broken money box behind the garages, with cheques flying all around.'

I agreed to drive him to the place that he had spoken of. Once there we found it to be just as he had said. I collected the cheques and the broken box and thanked God that there had not been any cash in the box that day. I was thankful to the person and to God for not losing any money. All was well in the end!

Towards the end of 2002, we as a family started to think about moving house to an area with better transport links to the city. Also there was talk of Wembley Stadium being rebuilt, which we thought would cause much local disruption. We debated the pros and cons of moving, but in the end decided to wait until it became clearer as to what would happen with the Stadium. My concern, however, of not moving too far away from the church was shared by both the vicar and the bishop. We went away on holiday to Pakistan in 2003 to have a break, before once again looking more seriously at the possibility of moving house.

On our return, we started looking in the North Harrow area, which has two tube stations close by, with good links to the city, and therefore seemed a good choice for a convenient commute into London. We found a house that we were interested in and arranged a viewing. On this very first visit we felt that this was the place for us. Also it was only a twenty-minute drive from the church when travelling outside peak hours. We met the owner there, who said that he was also a Christian and that he had been trying to sell the property for two years, but had been unable to do so. We felt God's hand in this, as it had been on our minds to move for these past two years. Very soon after this initial meeting we made an offer on the house, which was accepted after some negotiations. We moved into this house in North Harrow on 13th May 2004 (which is also, coincidentally, my birthday!).

At this point, I was running both the parent and toddlers' group and the after-school club alongside my church duties. 'What's next for me, Lord?' I asked. 'Please keep revealing Your will so I can keep everything in balance!'

11
Making Spaces

Eventually I found that all the regular involvement and travelling was becoming too much for me, and I felt that this might be a good time to review my current commitments. I needed to give myself some space, and perhaps in doing so, make space for others.

After running the parent and toddlers' group for around seven years, and after much deliberation, I decided to hand it over to another church member, who was a mother herself and who brought her own children to the group. She was happy to carry it forward. She interacted well with the children; each week she was already involved in leading a time of singing nursery rhymes, and getting the parents involved as well.

By this time the club was getting quite full, with grandmothers and local childminders also bringing children along. In this way, a strong connection was formed between the church and the parents and carers from the local community. It was encouraging for us to see, especially when some of them started to attend the church services on Sunday mornings, becoming regular church members, with their children also coming along to Sunday school.

One of the church members, who was also the after-school club committee chairperson, managed to register a breakfast club for the church as well. I ran the club for the first month or so, and when it had become established, I handed it over to one of the current staff members.

St James Church Centre is situated in the middle of a diverse community within Alperton. The vicar was very keen to try to reach out to the local community in different ways, and right from the beginning of my ministry there, he was encouraging me to start something for Urdu language speakers, such as a home group. After a few years, when I had fully settled into St James', the vicar asked me if I could begin a service in the Urdu language. Immigrants from various countries began to arrive, some as students and others with families, to settle here, and we had families who had to flee their countries of origin because of religious persecution. As their first language was not English, the vicar felt the need to start church services in their native languages.

I was initially reluctant to start a new fellowship, as I knew it would involve many challenges. However, I eventually agreed and helped to start up a combined service for Indians and Pakistanis, named the Hindi/Urdu Service. This fellowship was established in 2001 in the upstairs hall and later we moved into the main church.

I was assisted by Ajay More, an Indian member who was a committed Christian from Miraj, India, who had joined the church in 1999, alongside his wife, who was already a member of St James'. He had experience of preaching and leading worship with guitar from his church in India, and so he seemed the right person to join me in leading this fellowship.

Our service was conducted mainly in Urdu; we sang Urdu songs and Punjabi psalms. I had been brought up on the Punjab side of Pakistan, so Punjabi was my mother tongue. It was the native language of the Indians who left Pakistan after the Partition. I can speak Punjabi and can write down the Romanised version of the script, but cannot write in the original form, as Punjabi and Hindi are both difficult scripts to learn. I can read, speak and write in Urdu, but can only speak in Hindi.

The mixed language service was possible because the spoken languages are quite similar, having the same linguistic root, so Pakistanis and Indians could understand each other. Some families arrived from Pune, with their mother tongue being Marathi, which is entirely different in speech and handwriting from Hindi/Urdu. Yet they joined in the service and learned to sing and worship in each other's languages. The Scriptures could be read in Hindi and Urdu.

When growing up in Pakistan I studied in Urdu. I only studied English as a subject, and speaking English was not encouraged at all within the state schools. This is the reason I have had to work hard on improving my spoken English over the years and my vocabulary. This was greatly helped by listening to British radio, which I often have on while driving or when cooking.

For this new combined language service, we projected Romanised versions of the Hindi/Urdu/Punjabi languages onto a screen for those who could not understand the original scripts. Everyone sang and learned these songs and psalms. There was also a Sunday school catering for children of all ages, run by various church members. This was conducted in English as, for this second generation of children, English was now their first language.

Reflecting back on the mistakes made and to learn from them from the Hindi/Urdu service years and the difference of opinions we went through, it would have been better if we had used a mixture of Hindi, Urdu and Marathi songs and Scripture readings from the start in our adult church services. We could have avoided the problems that we encountered, with disagreements occurring over which languages were to be used during the service. Well, it's always good to learn from our mistakes! One needs to be open and generous when listening to others' opinions, as God works in different ways in different people's lives according to His perfect will. As it says in the book of Romans, 'We know that in all things God works for the good of those who love him, who have been called according to his purpose' (Romans 8:28).

Stanley always supported me fully in all the different areas of my ministry life. He operated the sound desk for the 9am service (and later did the sound at our 4pm service), where he worshipped in English as his Urdu reading is not great. I was only involved in leading the Hindi/Urdu service at this time. For me personally, leading the Hindi/Urdu service was a time to brush up on my spoken formalised Urdu and to grow in confidence when leading Asian services in other churches as well. Often I would switch between English and Urdu in the same service. We regularly had about thirty people attending the afternoon service; some were locals and others commuted from neighbouring areas. At Christmas and Easter some families travelled from east London, just to catch up with the community and to worship with us.

During my time with the Hindi/Urdu fellowship, we hosted two Christian concerts and two *Satsang* worship services. The Sanskrit term *Satsang* comes from two roots, *sat* which means 'true' and *sangha* which means 'community'. It was a sacred gathering, and leading the worship was a famous Indian convert from Bollywood, along with his wife, who had a powerful ministry among non-Christians. Congregations of Indians and Pakistanis were invited from all around London to join us. The worship time was Spirit-filled and encouraging for everybody present. Food was provided by our church members, and without knowing how many people would come, there was still plenty to go round, with more than 200 people attending in the end. Along with the enriching worship, it was a chance for Asian Christians from all over London to catch up with each other over the meal. This felt a bit like the miracle of the feeding of the 5,000!

We often had overseas ministers join us to preach and to share the news of their ministries, especially from India and Pakistan. Also, we hosted three worship concerts with local singers and invited congregations from Asian fellowships, which were well attended and supported. Food was donated by the Hindi/Urdu fellowship. After the afternoon service each Sunday, a different family would provide the refreshments, this time often becoming an excuse for family celebrations and extended times of togetherness.

One of our members, Dr Peter David, who is an activist for equal rights for minorities in Pakistan, had a passion to support less-privileged students in higher education there. Once he held one of many yearly fundraising functions at our church, which was well supported by both our fellowship and the Asian Christian communities around London. Traditional Asian food was served, as always, at the end of the evening.

To mark the five-year anniversary of the Hindi/Urdu fellowship in 2006 we had a large thanksgiving service at church, inviting all who had been involved during that time. After the service the vicarage garden was opened up to us, so that we could meet outside and share food together. The garden was decorated with Asian ornaments and other cultural displays for this occasion. It was a memorable event, enjoyed by all!

The opportunity to lead and to preach at the regular Sunday services was given to various members of the fellowship, especially on Good Friday, when traditionally there are seven short messages, one for each of Christ's seven statements from the cross.

This fellowship served as a training ground for many people and gave them the confidence to grow in their area of ministry. One member of the fellowship went on to be trained as a pastor to serve in the Moravian Church. My co-worker Ajay More from the Hindi/Urdu service also went on to become an ordained minister in the Church of England after three years of training. After being an ordained deacon for one year, he was priested in 2015 to serve as an associate vicar. Many more are now continuing to serve God in various ways, including leading choirs, Bible studies and public prayer and in music ministry.

After we moved house from Alperton to North Harrow in 2004 it felt like I was approaching another junction in my life. Should I find a job in a local after-school club? Or should I move to a church that was nearer to where we lived? It was a time of waiting upon God in prayer, allowing Him to show me the right way forward, because I was feeling quite drained and tired. Commuting back and forth for the Hindi/Urdu service every Sunday along with the daily after-school club was getting too much for me.

One day Stanley showed me the local newspaper and said, 'Here is a job being advertised for an after-school club coordinator.'

I replied, 'I am not looking for an after-school club job, only for a summer scheme role.'

A few days later he brought up the topic again. 'Well,' I said, 'there is no harm in applying!' I decided to fill in the form, as it was to be handwritten. During this process I had a strong feeling that the job would be mine. Through experience I have learned that this is one of the ways that God speaks to me, and sure enough, I got the job!

I resigned from St James' after-school club in 2005, but I carried on serving in the Hindi/Urdu service for another three years. Then I felt the time had come for me to move on from the Hindi/Urdu service also. There were issues that made leading the fellowship challenging for me, and I felt worn out from it all. Things were getting on top of me and I needed a break. I decided to leave in 2008. My colleague Ajay More was to continue as a leader, and it was renamed 'Christ for All Nations Fellowship'.

I was granted a substantial break from all church duties, returning to serve in the main English services when this time was over. I wondered what it would be like serving in English in the main church after such a long time. I was looking forward to this new chapter in my life.

12

New Shoots

Our daughter was well liked within our local Pakistani community and everyone was waiting expectantly for the time for her to get married. Some people told me that they were praying regularly for an appropriate partner for her to be found! One such person said to me that they would love to see Rebecca wed in their lifetime. By God's grace, all of our 'prayer warriors' lived to be able to celebrate with us at her wedding.

Stanley had been planning a trip to Pakistan to visit relatives in 2007 and our daughter, then thirty years old, decided to join him, intending to get some tailor-made Punjabi dresses while there. However, given her single status, the topic of potential future marriage partners was bound to crop up in conversations! In spite of a few recommendations from friends, no one suitable was found. I was getting a bit anxious about the whole situation.

While they were in Pakistan, I went to her room and was compelled to get down on my knees and stay in silence, knowing that God was concerned and knew the reason for my anxiety, whether I uttered any words or not.

After finishing, I felt a great peace and lightness in my spirit, knowing that my prayer had been heard. I could trust God, for His timing is always perfect. I stayed at peace, remembering that God cares for and loves her.

When she returned from Pakistan, I was encouraged to read 1 Corinthians 6:18-20 to her:

> Flee from sexual immorality. All other sins a person commits are outside the body, but whoever sins sexually, sins against their own body. Do you not know that your bodies are temples of the Holy Spirit, who is in you, whom you have received from God? You are not your own; you were bought at a price. Therefore honour God with your bodies.

I hoped that it may mean something to her in her future. In addition, words I heard from a church member made sense to me – these were that if both parties have marriage in mind, it is OK to meet up and get to know the potential suitor!

Eventually this right time came and everyone's prayers were answered. Rebecca's wedding became the highlight of the year within the Hindi/Urdu fellowship in 2008. Her husband, Soma, was a South African national, a convert to Christianity from Hinduism. The light of Christ initially came into his family when his elder sister, Kogila, decided to marry a Christian man, a son of a pastor. She subsequently decided to follow Jesus for herself, and their three children now serve with a church in Johannesburg, in various capacities.

Gradually the two others also decided to follow Jesus. His younger sister, Prabashni, met a man of Hindu origin who decided to explore Christian faith by attending church services with her. He began to find it interesting and something worth exploring further. After reading the Scriptures and studying for himself, he found truth in them and and baptised before their wedding day. Our son-in-law's middle sister, Saras, turned to Christ after a severe health scare and was healed after prayers by the church.

His mother, understandably, became concerned about all her children turning their backs on her Hindu religion. At one point during a visit to London, she shared this concern with me, saying, 'All my children are becoming Christians!' It sounded like it was a cause of great sadness to her.

A few years later, she was taken ill and was admitted to hospital. Visiting, members from the church would pray with her. The words must have stayed with her. She asked her younger daughter, Prabashni, to pray with her. Speaking on the phone, I also reassured her of our prayers for healing. She confessed Christ to her daughter, saying, 'I know now that Jesus died for my sins and I am forgiven.' Just a few days later she died.

Stanley and I flew to South Africa to attend her funeral. It was a beautiful service held at their local church. According to her instructions, South Indian food was to be served after the service. The church also provided a large variety of lovely food, in gratitude and honour to her as she often made large pots of traditional biryani for the church members to enjoy. It was an added honour for me that I was asked to take part in the final cremation service.

Her turning to Christ continued to affect others after her death, when one of her best friends dreamt that she was speaking to her, saying, 'There are many rooms in my Father's house.' Not knowing the Scriptures herself, the friend came to see one of the daughters of the lady who had died and was surprised to discover that these were the exact words Jesus had spoken to His disciples, as recorded in John's Gospel chapter 14 verse 2.

Our daughter was living with us in our home when she came to know about her husband-to-be Rebecca knew that she had our consent to meet and get to know someone if she liked him. I remember her once saying to me, while attending university, 'How can I get to know people unless I first meet with them?' When she told us about her interest in this man, Stanley asked if she was sure about her feelings for him. Her reply was, 'Over a time of getting to know each other, he has really grown on me.' On hearing this we were happy to give our blessing for her to continue to explore this relationship. Stanley and I met him on a number of occasions and grew to like him. It became clearer to us that the relationship was blossoming when she agreed to go to meet his mother and family – his father had died years before.

After a year or so, Soma came to us and asked us for Rebecca's hand in marriage, something we were happy to agree to. But she was not aware of him coming to us at this specific time. After a while, Rebecca phoned us to pass on the good news. She was surprised to find out that we already knew that he was going to propose!

Soma suggested a wedding date be set for the end of the year. As we were already in early June, Stanley was concerned about having such short notice (after all, Asian weddings don't come cheap!), but I showed my positivity and agreed to the idea, saying to Rebecca, 'Well, you are engaged now, so there is no point in delaying until next year.' His family agreed to travel from South Africa and Australia for the wedding.

The wedding itself was an occasion involving the whole St James Church. Soma, having foreign nationality, meant that the vicar had to first apply for a special licence to marry them in the church. The wedding service was to be held before sunset. My cousin from Canada was one of the witnesses. The reason we chose him was because his father had been one of the witnesses at our wedding.

The registration of the marriage was followed straight afterwards by a *mehndi* function in which henna is applied to the hands of the bride and groom by all the married women present, signifying a colourful, happy, long-lasting married life together. This sequence might seem a bit 'back to front' as normally the wedding ceremony happens after the *mehndi* function, and then the reception follows after that! The reason for it being this way was that the marriage service had to happen before sunset, when the vows were taken and the registers were signed. The *mehndi* celebration can happen late evening.

Many members of St James Church prepared and decorated the church hall. Homemade food was prepared and served to everyone. The following day we had a large wedding reception and blessing service with around 300 guests. During the speeches, Stanley contributed a few words, thanking everyone. He said, 'And now my wife will share a few words!' I just said whatever came to mind because I was not prepared at all. I must admit that I did get a bit emotional when talking about giving Rebecca away, leaving a bit of an uncomfortable silence, but everyone cheered and clapped, supporting me through the moment.

The wedding had been a great success. Nothing ever goes completely according to plan, but overall we were very happy with how things had gone. It was also a great joy to meet her new mother-in-law and the rest of the family for the first time. They brought fresh cultural diversity to our family, along with our new son-in-law and a brother-in-law for our son.

We were invited to go to South Africa for the reception party that was to be held for the rest of the family who could not join in the wedding in London. Stanley could not go, but I went, along with our son.

Since her marriage, our daughter has improved her cooking skills because of her husband's creative cooking! We often comment on his barbecue food, and how he combines South African and English herbs so well. We have told him that he would make an excellent chef in a top restaurant in London!

On one occasion Soma hurt his foot badly and was in plaster and on crutches for about three months. My earnest prayer for him – apart from the obvious need for a speedy recovery – was that God would be glorified and would fulfil His purposes during this rather frustrating time of convalescing at home. Surely God was in control of the situation, as we believe that God can use any of our circumstances for His glory, if we allow Him to do so with a humble attitude.

My prayers were answered in two ways. First, Soma recovered and was able to get a better job at a new company. I was extremely encouraged by God answering my prayers in this way. Soma had always worked hard and was very much a self-made man. Second, during this time of enforced incapacity, he became more dependent on God and learned to wait upon His timing. Praise God!

Our daughter was always a great help and a friend to me, especially when I needed to talk to someone. When she was about five, I told her, 'I am in trouble.' Her quick answer was, 'Jesus can help you.' Words coming from her meant a lot to me. We had entertained lots of guests at home. Her help was always needed making shish kebabs and rolling meatballs!

After their wedding, Soma and Rebecca moved into an apartment block in Greenwich, allowing them both easier access to their new places of work. Whenever they vacated the flat to go on holiday or the like, I would take the opportunity to go and stay there, enjoying having some time and space to myself for a while. A time to recharge my batteries!

In 2012, we had the joy of becoming grandparents for the first time. When it came close to the time for the baby's birth, it was found that she was positioned incorrectly and could not be turned, so a caesarean section was arranged. I stayed the night before with Rebecca at their home, so as to be able to be with her in the hospital the following day. From the ultrasound scans, we could see that everything else was fine, yet the thought would not leave me that something could still go wrong. What if the baby was not able to breathe or something was wrong with her lungs? The best thing I could do was to get down on my knees, to seek God's peace over this matter. When I did this, I received His peace and was able to leave it all in His hands. Perhaps God was using my concerns to draw me closer to Him, to be humble and to realise that I did indeed need to rely on Him for all things in life, and not to take anything for granted.

Before leaving for the hospital on the morning of the procedure, I put my hand where the baby's head was positioned and prayed for the safe delivery of a healthy child, thanking God for making us grandparents for the first time. Everything went well and Rebecca gave birth to a healthy baby girl. Thanks be to God!

Stanley and I enjoyed playing with our first grandchild and reading her stories, including ones from the Bible. One day, in 2014, I said to her, 'Tyler, you need to learn to love Jesus.'

Her answer was, 'How can I love someone if I don't know them?'

I was taken aback, amazed at how real and true her answer was, especially for someone of such a young age! Life is full of challenges, and all of us, including our children, have to face life bravely with God's help. I can carry on supporting and praying for my granddaughter and wait to see how God's work is accomplished in her life.

13
Growth Continues

My new job, joining an after-school club in a girls' school as coordinator while I was still a priest at St James', was a great challenge in my journey of faith. I was coming out of my comfort zone at St James' to a private school situated in acres of land. A large positive factor for me was that the school was run with a Christian ethos.

The club itself was situated in a separate house on the campus and so we could make use of the whole of the downstairs area. Having a caretaker close by was reassuring when the main school was closed after hours.

The club needed to be registered with OFSTED. That meant I needed to prepare a lot of files. I felt encouraged that God was with me and would guide me though this time. I knew that I needed to persevere when there were setbacks, allowing God to fulfil His plans, in His time, trusting that God does not make mistakes but rather always carries on His work to make us strong in Him. When working in a secular environment, I needed to remember that I was a priest, no matter where I was or what I was doing, and so should always act accordingly, with love and forbearance.

So often I hear of people leaving jobs because of difficulties they encounter. I think that if we are not happy in a certain place, we should not be too quick in deciding to quit; instead, we need to learn to face the challenges, and surely we will grow and mature through our trials.

One of the biggest lessons of life that I am learning is to take time to understand people's personalities, as every person is created differently – equal but not necessarily alike. We believe that everyone is 'fearfully and wonderfully made' (Psalm 139:14), in the 'image' and 'likeness' of God (Genesis 1:26-27). So I am trying to learn patience, not to get disheartened with people or circumstances, but rather to take some time and sleep on the matter. The next day may well bring a calmness and new perspective on the issue. After a few days have passed, God has often revealed new things to me, through His Word.

Working situations can be stressful; sometimes it is helpful just to pray, apologise and forgive if needed. The command to forgive is directed towards us first and foremost – see Colossians 3:13 – irrespective of how another person feels or reacts! And by this message, and our obedience to it, the gospel becomes alive within us. When Jesus was asked about the greatest commandment, He said that it was all about love, loving God and loving our neighbour, as we read in Matthew 22:36-40. He says elsewhere that we are to 'love each other as I have loved you' (John 15:12).

My new job was quite eye-opening for me. I came to know and work with staff from many different departments within the school, from all sorts of cultures and backgrounds. I took the opportunity to learn from their experiences and expertise, and I made some good friends! For me, the highlight of the year was the Christmas play put on by the nursery and reception children, where the girls played the characters from the nativity story. This was attended by the parents and families. The staff worked tirelessly to get the children ready to perform; it was a great joy to see everyone getting involved and hearing about the real meaning of Christmas.

After ten years based in the same building, in 2015 the club was relocated to the infant school. We now had to collect the children from different parts of the school, located in various buildings. I would need to get there a bit earlier before parents started arriving and taking up all the free space in the car park. On Wednesday mornings, when I had to take part in a midweek church service, I would sometimes grab my lunch from home and eat it in the car in the school car park just to be sure of getting a space!

Having access to a computer also became an issue as I no longer had my own office and so would have to wait until one was available, sometimes not until after five o'clock. After three years of working in the infants' school under these circumstances, I began to get a bit weary – this routine was getting to me. I began to consider retirement.

In many ways, 2018 was not a stress-free year. One issue was bed bugs. This may seem relatively trivial, but just try getting rid of them! I was the only one bitten. We tried all sorts of methods, even resulting in blasting the bedframe with a blowtorch in the garden, and yet they still remained! After many weeks like this, trying everything we could think of yet with no success, we eventually called in the experts and the job was done.

Then there was the time I was home alone when I noticed water coming from beneath our sink. When I investigated, I saw that there was a small leak in the water pipe. I tried to temporarily 'fix' the problem using adhesive, but this just made the problem worse! The water began gushing out faster than ever, flooding out onto the carpet. All I could do was attempt to catch the water using buckets, tubs and anything I could find, while spreading towels over the carpet. I tried to contact both Stanley and a plumber but could not get through to either of them. By now I was soaking wet and was beginning to panic! My mind was racing – where was I going to find help, and where in the house was our stopcock located? I reasoned that God would help, but how and when? The pool of water was growing!

I managed to contact one of my friends who suggested knocking at neighbours' doors to see if one of them could help. I felt that this was wise advice and worth a try. I was desperate anyway, so without wasting any more time I ran and knocked on our neighbours' door. To my great relief, I found that they were home. The first thing I was advised was to locate the stopcock, which I managed to do, and I managed to cut off the water flow to the house, thus alleviating the immediate emergency.

A few weeks later, Stanley started to feel unwell, and on the doctor's advice he was sent to hospital for further tests. After being at the hospital for some nine hours, he was eventually sent home, with a date for a follow-up appointment for an endoscopy. This revealed a problem within his stomach, for which he was prescribed some medication. However, a few days later his pain became unbearable, so we phoned the NHS 111 helpline. They told us to take him straight to the accident and emergency department of our local hospital. Once there, and after undergoing many further tests, he was diagnosed with gallstones. When I returned to the hospital the next day to visit, I was informed that they had found a blood clot in his spleen, and this needed to be dealt with before doing anything else. Subsequently my whole Easter break was spent visiting the hospital each day.

When the first day of the new school term arrived, Stanley was still in hospital and I felt strongly that this was the time for me to 'hang up my gloves' and retire from my after-school job while carrying on with church duties. The school management were very generous towards me, waiving my one-month notice period and even paying me for the whole month!

Our granddaughter, six years old then, was sad to see me going and asked, 'Do you have to leave?'

I told her, 'Yes, I must. I have worked long enough and am ready to retire now.'

Later, when I asked her about the after-school club, she replied, 'It's alright but it's different without you.'

At the end of the school year I was invited back to a farewell event, along with the other members of staff who had left during the year. I was given a traditional send-off with flowers, speeches, gifts and so on. This marked the end of my official working career.

I had a dream while Stanley was in hospital. In the dream I was in a large, old-style hospital ward and was standing next to Stanley's bed. At a distance I saw a very tall image of Jesus walking towards us. He was dressed in white robes, and four men who were almost half His size were walking with Him, two alongside Him, two behind. They had no wings – that's why I think that they were not angels![6] I could hardly believe my eyes. The whole ward was full of bright light, and I gazed upon them for a good few seconds. It was an awesome vision to treasure. I took this dream to be a sign of Stanley's future healing, and it was; after a year of treatment, including surgery, Stanley was finally given the all clear from the hospital in May 2019, having also had to recover from a bout of shingles during this time. Much later, Stanley decided to continue working, but on a semi-retired basis.

Having now both good health and more free time available, we took advantage of this opportunity and made a visit to the Holy Land. It was a soul-enriching experience for us, like going back in time to walk where Jesus walked and to see the Bible coming alive in front of our very eyes. The group of people we went with were very friendly and we quickly gelled together. The tour was led well and our guides were very knowledgeable, being able to answer all of our questions.

Our visit to the River Jordan was a memorable event. It was common for visiting pilgrims to get baptised there. I had always been reluctant to receive baptism by full immersion, because I had already been baptised as a child. I questioned the leader as to whether I would feel guilty if I received baptism again. She reassured me that I wouldn't. Stanley agreed to go ahead without any hesitancy, saying, 'We are here now – why don't both of

[6] Although Hebrews 13:2 implies that angels, when they appear to humans, do not always have wings!

us get baptised?' Normally when Stanley is unsure of something he will initially say 'No' to give himself time to think things through. But this time he was sure and we were both in agreement. I felt privileged to be immersed in the waters where Jesus was baptised. I was relieved that the wording on the certificates stated a rededication of our commitment.

After being immersed and coming up out of the water, I expected something special to happen. I kept my eyes closed and what I saw was a very smooth pyramid shape covered with ivory-coloured smooth tiles. I kept my eyes focused on it, just to make sure that it was real. I thought the river where I was actually standing might be surrounded by mountains, but on opening my eyes there were just green trees all around. My own interpretation of this vision was that my life ahead might seem smooth initially, but as I climb further on I must be aware of slipping back down, and for this I need perseverance and a trust in God for whatever comes my way. He will help me to reach the top of the pyramid one day.

14
Plant Concerns

Most of us can relate very well to the character of the prodigal son in Luke 15, along with many other characters in the Bible. Their fallibility reminds us that they failed, but when they repented, they were forgiven and accepted by God.

In the parable, the younger son took advantage of the free will given to him by his father. He had the privilege of staying with his father or rebelling and going his own way. Upon his request, the father, who represents God in this story, gives him his share of the inheritance. The son was very happy and off he went, spending the money on whatever his heart desired. However, after all the money was spent, he became destitute and accepted a job looking after pigs, and he became very hungry.

When he came to his senses and thought of the comfort at his father's house, he decided to return home, intending to say to his father, 'Father, I have sinned against heaven and against you. I am no longer worthy to be called your son; make me like one of your hired servants' (Luke 15:18-19). So he started back on his journey towards his father, but 'while he was still a long way off, his father saw him and was filled with compassion for him; he ran to his son, threw his arms round him and kissed him' (v20). The son repeated the decided words to his father. His father, however, called for his servants and instructed them to bring fine clothes for him and to prepare a feast in order that they might celebrate his son's return.

Why am I discussing this parable here? Well, I have in mind my son and the way his life was turned round for the better, after losing his way in his youth. I remember in the early 1990s at St James Church, a visiting speaker spoke to young mothers about how to train our children to be responsible for their actions when they were old enough. My daughter was a teenager at that time, and my son a little younger. One example was to give them their own alarm clock, to allow them to take responsibility to get up for school on time; also to give them their uniform and allow them to dress themselves. If they ended up late for school then they must bear the consequences! Our job was to raise them up as responsible citizens by giving some space, trusting and reassuring them that we would always be there when they needed us. My own children were older by then but still I learned something new! I believe learning never stops at any age. With the fast-changing world, we need to keep upgrading our knowledge.

Learning from their own mistakes can and might help children to grow towards maturity. I took these basic principles on board and they stayed with me for the rest of my life. Being an immigrant, I needed to watch and learn to practise the right principles for my own life from the previous generation, from work colleagues and church fellowship. Looking back over the years, I can't say how strictly I kept to these principles, but I do know that both of our children had the liberty, within limits, to explore life for themselves.

Being a young mother and new to the country, maybe I kept a bit of a close eye on them, but understandably, as this was part of my culture. St James' was the one and only church for me to learn and to grow for my entire ministry. It was the same for my children as well.

Stanley liked to travel and explore new places. We had many fun family holidays together with them, including going to Niagara Falls – the wonder and the beauty of God's world was much appreciated by us all. I assume our children inherited the habit of travelling from Stanley; I am just a follower as far as travelling is concerned.

Things did not play out quite as smoothly as was expected in our son's life. Even so, I had peace, knowing what the Scriptures tell us in one of my favourite verses: 'And we know that in all things God works for the good of those who love him, who have been called according to his purpose' (Romans 8:28). His Christian name is Sharoon; it is the name given to the Valley of Sharon in the Urdu Bible translation. We can find this name in Isaiah 65:10: 'Sharon will become a pasture for flocks, and the Valley of Achor a resting-place for herds'. This is a prophecy given to Isaiah by God for the nation of Israel.

In the early 1980s the name Sharoon was quite popular in Pakistan. The name was suggested by Stanley's aunt who was visiting us from Pakistan at the time of his birth. His nickname also came from her suggestions. (While mentioning the origins and meanings of names, I would add that the meaning of my name is 'hard-working'. I must say that I do indeed fit into this category. Sometimes

I do too much, so that my energies are completely drained, and this then makes me reflect upon my given name!)

There are stories of my life that connect with my journey of faith. I was referred to St Mary's Hospital in London for investigations around the reasons for not being able to conceive. At that time my monthly cycle was very erratic. After an initial test, I received the surprising news that I had already conceived and so no further appointments were needed! We were both very happy to hear this good news, and thanked God for His mercies.

Another related story comes from when I was in my eighth month of pregnancy. I was attending a house group prayer meeting. Afterwards, a lady sitting beside me said, 'Last night I dreamt that the woman sitting next to me is going to have a baby boy.' This was news to us, as at that time nobody was allowed to be informed about the sex of their baby. Another pointer for us was that on our way to the hospital, on my expected due date, the car in front of us had a number plate with the word 'son' written within it. We took it as a confirmation that this lady's dream might well come true, and so it proved to be!

Twice during his childhood, Rocky narrowly avoided being hit by a car. On one occasion, when he was barely two years old, he managed to get out onto the road just outside our house. The first I knew about it was when I heard the screeching of car brakes. I rushed outside and saw him standing in the middle of the road just inches away from the bonnet of a car. I scooped him up into my arms, just thankful that he was OK.

The second incident occurred on the same stretch of road, when he was about eight years old. He was playing football with his friends on the pavement. The ball must have gone into the road, and the boys chased after it. The driver of an approaching car had to slam down on his brakes so hard in order to stop that his car actually spun around. Amazingly, none of the boys got hurt. Looking back now, I can see God's protective hand has always been upon my son.

After completing his school education he went on to college where he studied graphic design and got his BTEC diploma. He then went on to study product design, but after two years he dropped out. He chose to do this because he did not see a future for himself in that field. Eventually he decided to pursue a career in electrical installation, training at the City of Westminster College. He took an apprenticeship, working with a company for eight years while gaining experience. Then he joined in a partnership with good friends.

At times when he did not have a job, he was out and about with friends till late at night. Whenever he came home, I felt a great sense of peace coming over me. I had no questions to ask.

Truthfully, I spent times worrying about my son. But God's peace assured me that all would be well. Being brought up in a Christian home, he always believed in the power of prayer. He often asked me to pray for him when he could not sleep. He had good teaching from Sunday school, confessed his faith and was confirmed. I believed that the seed of faith had been sown and nurtured. Maybe the hope of bearing fruit one day gave me peace about him.

15
Ripening Fruits

Now, it might seem like an old Asian tradition for parents to get involved in arranging their children's marriages! I believe it can be common in the first generation... Call it losing my patience or not keeping my eyes open, but I began to wonder, 'Where am I going to find a wife for Rocky?'

I have always believed that God is in control of everything. He has not let me down so far. Whenever I am down, He lifts me up, staying true to His promise, 'Never will I leave you; never will I forsake you' (Hebrews 13:5).

It was late at night when my mind started to work like a computer, googling around the worldwide web, looking for a suitable partner. Suddenly I was reminded of Stanley's cousin's widow, Rani, who had been calling me from Pakistan occasionally over the past year. She had a daughter, Sonia, for whom she was looking to find a husband. The conditions were that he needed to be of good character, hard-working and from a good Christian family. I had told her that I would keep an eye out, but had not previously thought about this match for Rocky!

Sonia's father, who was Stanley's cousin, had been a pageboy at our wedding. In the past, when her mother had been getting anxious about sorting out Sonia's future marriage partner, Stanley had eased her mind, telling her that whoever she chose, we would be there for her to help arrange things.

I became excited and thought to myself, 'I may have got my answer from God!'

I got up early the next morning and called Rani, asking, 'Have you found anyone yet for Sonia?' Hearing her answer in the negative, I said, 'Just pray about the situation,' but I did not mention Rocky to her at this time.

A few months later, I visited Pakistan, and while there, I stayed with my sister in Lahore, coincidently where Sonia's family also lived! One afternoon my sister, her husband and I met up with Sonia's family for tea. We all liked the girl but left without saying anything about a possible future match, as Rocky knew nothing of our thoughts at this stage.

On my return to London, I spoke to Rocky about her, but he did not seem interested in talking about it. Eventually he asked me to give him two years, then he went to work. Obviously, it would be the biggest decision of his life, so we left all of this in God's hands, believing that He would work it out in His time, if it was right for both of them.

After a year or so, I thought that maybe the girl could visit the UK over Christmas, to experience London (and to meet up). Culturally, for this to go ahead, to reassure her mother that her daughter would be looked after by us as if she were our own daughter, we asked for her hand in marriage to Rocky. Everyone in her family was happy to hear of this proposal, but sadly her tourist visa request was rejected. Sonia and Rocky agreed to communicate online in order to get to know each other better. This continued for a year and by that point Rocky felt more at peace and happy, and was ready to move forward with this new relationship.

Sonia and Rocky decided to meet up with each other at a destination where Sonia could more easily get a visa to visit. After this meeting, they were both happy to go ahead with the marriage. The wedding date was set for the summer of 2015, when Rocky would be thirty-two years old, with the ceremony to be held in Lahore, Pakistan. The timing of this was convenient for me as it fell within my summer break from school, as I was still employed in the after-school club at that time. It did mean that we would be there during the hottest time of the year, but we felt that the timing was right and trusted God in this decision.

Initially there were going to be three functions in total, but a fourth one was later added by Sonia's family, to be held in their own place before the wedding. This was the *mayoon* function that involves close family and friends anointing the bride and groom with oil upon their foreheads – as Christians, we make a sign of the cross here. *Mehndi* (henna) is also placed on their palms, signifying a happy future. There was colourful bunting hung up all around and we entered to the sound of the beating of the *dole* (drum) accompanied by a shower of rose petals. There was also delicious traditional food served afterwards. Having mentioned these traditions, which have their origins from within Indian culture, I can say that personally I don't find any particular Christian significance to them, apart from the anointing with oil in the name of the Lord Jesus in the form of a cross.

As soon as I broke up for the summer from school, I travelled over to Pakistan. Stanley came soon afterwards, followed by Rocky a few days later, accompanied by some of his close friends. Our daughter arrived just before the wedding functions began. In God's provision, a long-term good friend, Abid, opened his house to us. He had travelled from Singapore with his wife and daughter, especially for this occasion. It was a real blessing to be able to stay with him and his family during this period. Their house was equipped with all the modern facilities and was fully air-conditioned. We were given the use of his car and driver to transport us around the area. Their personal chef was always on hand to cook for us and their in-house maid took care of all the cleaning and laundry jobs.

The engagement ceremony was actually held in the front garden of Abid's house, in a marquee. They were already verbally engaged, without a ring, but this was a kind of publicly announced engagement, celebrated with rings in the presence of the family and friends. This generally happens in arranged marriages with the blessings of the priest, and prayers.

The décor was closely supervised by our friend, and a lavish buffet was prepared by his chef. As a gift, his family provided all the dresses that Sonia and I needed for all of the wedding functions, as well as many other precious gifts. They were keen for all the functions to go well. It was owing both to their contacts in Lahore and their love for us that everything proceeded so smoothly and with great success.

The marriage ceremony was conducted at Lahore Cathedral Church of the Resurrection, built by the British government in 1887. The service was conducted by the dean, and the preacher was the Bishop of Lahore. At our request, our friend Abid agreed to be the witness signatory on the marriage certificate from our side of the family, Sonia's uncle being the other signatory. Sonia was given away by the good friend of her late father, Russell Emanuel, fulfilling her father's wishes. He travelled to Pakistan specially to attend the wedding. Many of our relatives travelled from all over Pakistan to join us in the city of Lahore.

One of Rocky's concerns was the very high temperatures likely during the summer period. The temperatures often rise to more than forty degrees! However, we were blessed with rain, cool breezes and temperatures of not more than thirty-two degrees. As soon as we returned to the UK, a heatwave hit Lahore, with temperatures soaring to well above forty degrees. I see this as God's hand at work, blessing us during this time.

Not all went according to plan, though! On the day of the *mehndi* celebration, Sonia was at a beauty parlour about an hour's drive away from the function hall. She had written down the address of the beauty parlour, which ended with the line, 'Block xx', but when this was relayed to her driver it was assumed the 'xx' were kisses, so this information was omitted. Time passed, the driver couldn't find her, his phone battery had died, Sonia's phone battery was also dead, the beauty parlour closed, the staff went home and Sonia was left outside with the security guard! On top of it all, the heavy rains made traffic worse and caused more delays.

While our guests waited and waited, food was served to save time, and eventually the bride arrived at the *mehndi* party some three hours late! All of the dances and *mehndi* customs were completed in the final hour of our celebration. No one was any the wiser as to all the panic that had gone on behind the scenes!

Another incident occurred. One of our friend's vehicles was stolen from the front of the house. I understand it's not uncommon anywhere in the world to have vehicles stolen, but obviously it was shocking and unbelievable that it could have happened, especially on the day of the wedding. While I was sitting at the family breakfast table with his wife, Abid walked in with the news of the theft, and I had a strong inner conviction that the vehicle would be recovered by the evening. This seemed too good to be true. Perhaps I should have said something to him right there, but I realised that it was a big claim to make, and what if it didn't come true?

Even before the wedding reception was over, the news was announced that the vehicle had been recovered. It had been involved in a minor accident and could not be driven any further in that condition, though it was repairable. I regretted so much not trusting the sweet small voice of the Lord to me.

When all the wedding celebrations were over, we returned to the UK with happy hearts and praised the Lord. Rocky settled back into his work routine, now needing to save up enough money to apply for the spouse visa required for Sonia to come and join him here. Although the first application was rejected for lack of some paperwork, the second time the visa was granted. They were united again after two years – a long wait.

The couple made a choice to live with us. Equally, it was Stanley's wish that they stayed with us. This again is very much part of our Asian culture, to live together in an extended family unit. There seemed to be a lot of adjustments that needed to be made. We all have rough edges that need to be smoothed! We needed to learn to live together with respect and with an understanding of each other's needs. As a family, we like to be able to be there for each other.

Sonia settled in well, learning the differences between the way we do things in the UK and in Pakistan. Maybe it was easier for her to adjust to life in the UK than it was for me, as the world is much smaller now, and our cultures are not as far apart as they once were. She brought her own style of cooking, using strong spices, and she and I happily shared the cooking duties together. It was a great blessing that Sonia was able to get a good office-based job. We felt blessed to have them around, making us a complete family.

Sometime after we moved into our current house, we had rebuilt the old garage, converting it into a small bedroom with an en-suite bathroom. My initial thoughts were that maybe we could have somebody live with us, such as a foreign student, who might also be able to help me out with the cooking and so on when we had people to stay. I had some individuals in mind but this never came to pass, the space more commonly being used to accommodate visitors. After Sonia's arrival, I came to realise that my prayers for help had been answered – not in the way I had envisaged, but rather in God's way.

God has provided me with much more than I asked for. It was worth the wait and perseverance.

In time, Rocky and Sonia were blessed with the gift of a baby son, Leon. The baby was initially placed into an incubator for a few days while further tests were carried out. This was a concerning time for us, made worse by the fact that we could not see him; only the father was allowed to be in the hospital. All we could do was pray and trust God. I remember our granddaughter joining with us in prayer. She dragged my prayer desk out into the lounge, placed the crucifix on top and lit a candle. She got down on her knees. 'Lord Jesus,' she said, 'heal Leon so he can learn to love You.' When the day of Leon's homecoming finally arrived, she took the lead in putting up banners and balloons. I thanked God for the happy ending.

Leon is growing well now and is a healthy little boy. He has become the joy of our lives! Stanley and I notice each and every little change as he grows. Maybe we were too busy to notice and enjoy such changes when our own children were growing up. It is said that grandparents are around to enjoy and to spoil the grandchildren, and certainly we find that to be true.

Leon is a French name, meaning lion. The lion in many cultures symbolises kingliness, grandeur and courage. His middle name, David, means 'beloved', and is the name of the great biblical king.

With Leon's arrival we feel very much a full family. He has brought added joy into our home and he is good company for me, keeping me fully occupied! Being brought up in a large family, the family unit is very close to my heart. Maybe that's why we have always welcomed visitors and students to stay with us in our house over the years.

I started the previous chapter by talking about the parable of the prodigal son. I could see some parallels between his story and that of our son's life. I praise God for now seeing him settled back into the routine of a family life. He is a God-fearing Christian and would love to see his son growing up in the faith of Lord Jesus.

God is much bigger and greater than my limited understanding of Him.

16
Hearing the Gardener

Throughout this book, as I have told you my story, I have used gardening terms for the titles of the chapters. Here I want to talk about knowing the Gardener. We need understanding to discern the difference between hearing our own inner voice and hearing the voice of God.

The question for me was, 'How can I know God's voice and guidance unless I have a real, ongoing relationship with Him?' I needed to be like one of the sheep we read of in John 10; she recognises her shepherd's voice and can tell when it is not her Master calling (vv4-5).

By regularly reading and studying the Scriptures, I came to some rough guidelines.

- First, I need to start each day in an attitude of repentance; asking forgiveness for my daily shortfalls and asking for God's grace to overcome them.

- Second, I should aim to read and meditate on the Scriptures, to learn about the life stories of God's people and their walk with or without God.

- Third, I need the wisdom to know 'the mind of Christ' (1 Corinthians 2:16), to learn about His purpose and plan and the right time for answered prayers.

- Fourth, I need to understand about the fruit of the Holy Spirit, and to incorporate this into my life. As it says in Galatians 5:22-23, 'The fruit of the Spirit is love, joy, peace, forbearance, kindness, goodness, faithfulness, gentleness and self-control.'

- Fifth, I need to stand firm in the faith of Christ, actively choosing to stand on the 'Rock of [my] salvation' (Psalm 95:1), who is the 'Beginning and the End' (Revelation 21:6; 22:13), 'who is, and who was, and who is to come' (Revelation 1:4, 8).

- Sixth, I need to learn to rest in the peace that Jesus gives, being reassured that He is with me, in every situation, 'to the very end of the age' (Matthew 28:20). He says, 'Peace I leave with you; my peace I give you. I do not give to you as the world gives. Do not let your hearts be troubled and do not be afraid' (John 14:27).

- Seventh, I need to identify which gifts from the Scriptures I have; how can I develop them to share with the Church family?

Over the years of walking in faith, and making mistakes, it has got a bit easier to distinguish between my own thoughts and what God might be saying. It has come with the practice of not rushing to do things without waiting. It has come with the trial and error of years of practice.

It was common with me to miss the sweet small voice of God – just like the prophet Samuel who, as a boy, lying down to sleep in the temple, mistook the Lord's voice for that of Eli the priest. We read in 1 Samuel 3:2-10 that he did this three times, before coming to understand that it was the Lord Himself speaking to him!

It is also true that unless I first know who I am in Christ and have a strong, firm relationship with Him, then I cannot know how to relate properly to other people, to know how to love, forgive and build healthy relationships with them.

The Christian message as I have understood it begins with the call of John the Baptist. His message was that God's judgement upon the world was imminent and that, to prepare for this judgement, all people need to repent of their sins, be baptised and 'produce fruit in keeping with repentance' (Matthew 3:8).

To know God through Jesus Christ, we need to build a living relationship with Him. If we believe that Jesus is alive, and that He is 'the same yesterday and today and for ever' (Hebrews 13:8), then we must believe that He is here with us, among us, around us and in us by His Holy Spirit. He can hear our prayers and is able to answer. Most of the time we are quick to bring prayers to God for our needs and then, without waiting to hear from Him and know His answer, we go ahead and do whatever we wanted to do in the first place!

I would like to share some stories from my life that illustrate how I have come to know God and learned to hear His voice more clearly over the years.

I remember an occasion from my teenage years when my brother was standing on the rooftop next to the surrounding wall. There was a small piece of a brick close to him that was loose. When I looked up at him, the thought came to my mind that the piece of brick could fall on my grandmother who was sitting just below him. The very next moment, the brick fell, bounced off the washing line and just grazed her head! I realised that this could have been much worse, and wondered why I hadn't warned them earlier. On reflection, though, there had been only a split second to speak up before the brick fell.

I promised myself there and then that the next time I had such a premonition, I would speak up sooner. In more recent years, such warnings have come to me with a longer gap before their fulfilment. I have been keeping quiet about this gift for a long time, but now, with God's grace, I know for sure that it is from Him.

On another occasion, our house in Alperton was burgled, with the intruders entering via the kitchen door. I knew that the small window next to the door had a loose handle. For three nights beforehand, while locking up, I had stood next to it and thought to myself that a burglar could push the window inward and be able to open the door, as I always left the key in the lock. However, I did nothing about it. And lo and behold, the house was burgled within that week!

God has often granted me 'the desires of [my] heart' (Psalm 37:4). My wanting to visit London when I was younger and then ending up moving here to live is just one such example. Perhaps this desire to visit London was given to me by God, in order for me to be able to fulfil His calling on my life later on.

Over the years, I came to know this God who longs to have a heart-to-heart relationship with His people. Many times, when I have had a desire in my mind, I have been surprised by God, who, in His timing and in a better way than I could have planned, and without me having to do anything to bring it about, has met my need. For example, not long ago, after collecting some points on a reward card, I decided to treat myself to a bottle of a nice perfume. Then someone I know who loves perfumes came to me. She handed me a large bottle of perfume! This might seem like a trivial example, but I know that God cares, even in such simple ways.

During my younger life at home, I learned obedience, trying to abide by my mother's instructions humbly, and I taught my siblings to do the same. I believe this was the beginning of my learning to respect and obey others. As it says in the Ten Commandments, 'Honour your father and your mother, so that you may live long in the land the LORD your God is giving you' (Exodus 20:12).

I believe that obeying God is good, healthy and less stressful than living in disobedience! I would like to share here one incident of when I did not stop to pray nor waited to listen to God, but went ahead in my own strength.

While I was in Pakistan in 1979 there was a terrorist attack on the American embassy, and so my flight for London was cancelled and I had to look for alternative ways of getting back. I learned my lesson from this incident. Since then, before making any plans to travel, I pray, wait upon God, and don't fly until I get a positive answer! I try to always wait on God to know what I should do. I am learning to make it my habit to wait for God's answer before making any big decisions.

It is also in the Scriptures that God speaks to us through dreams, as He did with Joseph and other prophets, and you will know from my story so far that I am a great believer in dreams.

Lastly, I have learned the importance of forgiveness. I need to forgive as God has forgiven me in Jesus, as it says in Ephesians 4:32. And not to worry, bringing all my cares to God. It states in the book of Philippians:

> Do not be anxious about anything, but in every situation, by prayer and petition, with thanksgiving, present your requests to God. And the peace of God, which transcends all understanding, will guard your hearts and your minds in Christ Jesus.
> (Philippians 4:6-7)

I wonder where the Lord will lead me next, with the experience of knowing Him a little better.

17

New Ways of Sowing

With the vicar, John Root, retiring in 2011, St James', like any other church, was left with a large hole to fill. One of the curates covered the one-year interregnum period. After this time, we were blessed with the appointment of joint vicars, a husband and wife, Rev Steve and Rev Ali Taylor. This was to be a job share, with them both working part-time, together completing a full position. They both brought their own gifts and personalities to the role, enriching the spiritual life of St James'.

It was a time of big change for St James' after many years of being led by our previous vicar. It was a lot to come to terms with – new management, new ways of running the church and moving on with God's plan. People often get used to certain ways of leadership; it can take some time for the congregation to adjust to new ways. Ultimately, not everyone is going to be happy about changes. I believe, though, that this is how God's plan is fulfilled in the life of the Church, when His called ones are sent to serve and to use their talents and gifts in the appointed places.

At the time of John Root's retirement, I initially thought that it might be good for me to explore whether I should transfer to my more local church. For me it was once again a time to wait upon God, to search for His will. Did He want me to stay at St James' or was it time for a move? I explored this issue with the new leadership and it was agreed that I needed some time to think and pray about it, until I felt sure of where I should be.

After speaking with our area dean, the bishop arranged for me to visit a local church to attend services and to meet the vicar there who was due to retire in the not-too distant future. I received a warm welcome from the congregation and the churchwardens, but I was not sure if this church was the right fit for me. The more I thought about it, the more I felt unsure that this was the right move. The church was only five minutes' drive away instead of the twenty minutes to reach St James', but on the other hand there would be lots of adjustments to make. It would be like starting from scratch, with new people, new management, different ways of doing things, and I was not sure that I was up to it! At this point in time I was still working part-time at the after-school club every weekday afternoon.

I met again with the new leadership, the joint vicars, to see if they would still want me at St James' and was assured that there was still a role for me there. After much thought and prayer, I made up my mind to stay, so I met up with them once again and gave my decision. At that moment, as described in the last chatper, the 'joy of the LORD' (Nehemiah 8:10) came over me. I began to laugh as I never had before. It seemed to be a positive sign from the Lord. I thanked God for His guidance and leading. I was completely sure that I was at the right place to continue to serve for the rest of my ministry.

Preaching has never been my strongest gift. I always saw it as an opportunity to increase my own biblical understanding when studying for sermons. I prepared them with the best of my knowledge of Scripture, also drawing on my own personal relationship with the Lord. I often added examples of other people's personal experiences of walking with the Lord, so as to make the Scriptures alive and relevant. Planning sermons did not come naturally to me, but I adopted the habit of meditating on the passages, praying for my mind to be opened to what God was saying to us at St James', then I would consult commentaries or a study Bible and begin to write my introduction. The rest seemed to flow from there.

In light of the increased ethnic diversity in St James Church borough, the spiritual needs of the area have thus changed significantly as immigrants from other religious backgrounds have also increased. The new vicars were placed in St James' as they have a heart for cross-cultural ministries and evangelism. At the time of writing, the vicars have had increased contact with the local Hindu temple, visiting them at times of Christian and Hindu festivals, meeting the people and sharing the good news of Jesus Christ.

One effective area of ministry has been a form of street evangelism, called Healing on the Streets. It's like taking the church out in the streets, before inviting people into the church. The idea came from the ministry of Jesus, where He went around healing and casting out demons, which was a sign of His victory over the evil powers. We, as His followers, want to continue His ministry, proclaiming His power to heal and overcome evil spirits.

Hence, a group from St James' began to meet weekly at a regular location. Along with singing and worship music, people came forward to receive prayer for healing. The prayers were offered according to each person's needs, which varied from minor aches and pains to bigger spiritual issues. Then they were given the choice to come to church for further prayer and more understanding about the life and work of Jesus. This ministry proved fruitful, with many people being baptised and becoming part of the church, many settling into our afternoon Hindi language service, and Gujarati speakers meeting at 9pm for Bible study and prayers. Most of the converts were Gujarati speakers but also spoke and understood the Hindi language. I saw this outreach as a step forward for St James Church, being built on the previous initiatives and evangelism projects that began many years ago under the ministry of previous leadership. It still continues at the time of writing.

To mingle and to get to know each other better, the various congregations worshipped together once a month. Worship songs were translated to and from English, Hindi and Tamil. This way everyone could join in with the singing, or at least read the words in their own language.

In September 2019, St James' trialled holding a 'café church' service, where all the congregations could meet for breakfast at 10am once a month. This was followed by a short talk, discussion questions around tables, craft activities, sung worship and Holy Communion. People were encouraged to share tables with other members from other services and also to invite 'unchurched' friends. This carried on until March 2020 when the coronavirus pandemic hit Britain.

Alongside my priestly duties, I was asked to coordinate the seniors' ministry in the church. There were six of us altogether in the team. Some of the team members had full-time jobs and I mostly visited with those available. I was always grateful to those who served joyfully and diligently to make our seniors' Christmas party a delightful occasion for all those who attended. There were some twenty seniors on the church electoral roll who could be visited at home or sometimes in hospital. We would offer them home Communion and on occasions when requested would have the privilege to pray over them the last rites. I knew in my heart that this was an important part of my ministry, to serve the vulnerable and the housebound. I connected well with such people; I was able to be a link between them and the church.

In these special moments we were able to bring real joy and see smiles on their faces. In performing this ministry, I felt that it was our turn to serve our senior church members, just as they had served the church over many years previously. We also remembered to acknowledge their birthdays by celebrating with them, bringing cakes and flowers. This act of love and kindness was always well received.

The most encouraging times for us were when, along with their carers, some of their family members joined us for home Communion services. Although many did not partake in the sacrament – maybe they were not committed Christians – it was still a joy to have them with us. We left the rest up to the Lord! After all, it is the work of the Holy Spirit to make the seed grow. Some of our seniors had developed dementia, yet when we took home Communion to them they were still able to join in with the confession and prayers, having learned them by heart.

A memorable event from this period was the celebration at St Paul's Cathedral marking twenty years since women were first ordained priests in the Church of England. I felt greatly supported by St James', with our vicars and many of the congregation making a special effort to join me at the service. The seating was limited and many of the church members were not able to get a space inside St Paul's itself. I was very touched by the fact that despite this they chose to stay and watch the service relayed on a big screen instead.

Afterwards, a large group of us were photographed with the Archbishop of Canterbury on the steps of St Paul's. This was especially poignant as on the day when we had been ordained we had not been allowed to gather on the steps for an official photograph, owing to fears of reprisals from those gathered there to oppose the ordination of women priests. To mark the occasion, St James' presented me with a home Communion set, which was something I had always wished for. Also, I was given a white stole patterned with lilies, which went well with the liturgical robes that I wore for special occasions.

Time flew quickly before I realised it was the time for the silver jubilee, celebrating twenty-five years of the priesting of women! By then we had a new Bishop of London, the first-ever female bishop, Dame Sarah Mullally. The whole service was organised very thoughtfully, with various women priests sharing their experiences of the last twenty-five years of ministry, serving in their communities. Again, many from St James' joined me in celebrating the day at St Paul's.

In the weeks following, St James' organised a 'bring and share' lunch after one of our communal services to celebrate women's priesting. Here, all four congregations were together. This involved each family taking time to cook or make something to share with the whole church. My ten-year-old niece baked a large cake for the occasion, decorated with silver icing, which I could cut and share with all present to celebrate this occasion. I invited my family and friends to join us for the service and for the food afterwards. I celebrated Holy Communion on the day using wine that I had brought back from the Holy Land, after our trip there, which had been produced in Cana of Galilee. This is the place where Jesus had performed His first miracle of turning water into wine, which we read about in John 2. It was received joyfully with grateful hearts by the whole congregation.

I had been serving in the Church of England for twenty-eight years. Looking back even further to 1987, when I was accepted at Oak Hill Theological College, my heart filled with joy and awe at the graciousness of the Lord, who had sustained me over all these years. He had kept me moving forward even though I had not always known what He had in store for me. Right from the beginning, the Lord had been opening doors for me, and help had always been at hand from colleagues and friends.

I now felt ready to move on with the next phase of my life, as I began to consider formal retirement from my duties as priest… though I knew one never really retires from serving God! I knew that once again I would need to wait upon God for His guiding hand and for His future plans to unfold.

It goes without saying that without Stanley's support none of this journey would have been possible. He has supported me at every step, both practically and financially. He is the unsung hero of this book, chosen by God for His purpose to be fulfilled in my life. This does not mean that God's work in me has been fully accomplished; I believe that it has only just begun!

18
Handing Over to the Gardener

Whenever I was asked the question about retiring from my priestly duties, either by one of my appointed appraisers or by the bishop, I often wondered to myself, and would reply, 'I am not so sure about the right time.' Maybe I could just not imagine stopping. What would be my focus for the days ahead if I was no longer serving as a priest, visiting people or studying the Scriptures while preparing my sermons? After all, I had often felt a little bit lost during the school holidays when I did not have to work at the after-school club, so how would I feel now?

I was told by church colleagues that getting used to the new routine of retired life could take more than a year. I had experienced something similar when I had stepped down from the after-school club. Also, I knew that staying spiritually strong would be another challenge, as I am not one of those people who have the habit of regularly reading or studying without being given a specific task.

Although I had been officially ministering on a part-time basis, with not much overall responsibility within the church, I realised that incumbent ministers generally retire by the age of seventy. When speaking with the bishop during my last appraisal, he confirmed that if my health was fine then I could carry on ministering in my current capacity until the age of seventy, which would be in 2022. At this point, I would cease to be a non-stipendiary minister, but I could apply for 'Permission to Officiate' (PTO), and so could continue with some priestly duties on a more ad hoc basis.

As time went by, I felt that my energy levels were starting to decrease. I was missing many evening church meetings as I found it increasingly uncomfortable to drive at night. I kept up with my responsibilities of leading and preaching at daytime church services while coordinating the seniors' ministry, but I knew that I needed to slow down a bit. When I told the vicars that I was going to write my memoir, they kindly took me off the preaching rota for a while, so that I could concentrate on my writing.

The thought of retiring was becoming stronger and stronger within me. After celebrating Holy Communion for one of the services, I thought the time was right to talk to the vicars about it. They listened and said they would keep this issue in prayer. The following Wednesday, after the midweek service, one of the vicars approached me and said, 'After praying about it, both of us feel peace about your retirement. Whenever you are ready, please let us know and inform the bishop's office as well.'

This would be the fourth time in my working life that I had resigned from a position. The first was my job with the contact lens company. Interestingly, the last three times had been with very short notice or no notice at all. The first was St James' after-school club, the second was the other after-school club and the third was from ministry in St James Church. I always thought that I would know well in advance when it would be right for me to retire from church ministry, but once again it came all of a sudden.

As it turned out, one Sunday was my last official service. By then we all had to take extra precautions when at church, to help combat the COVID-19 pandemic, which had begun in early 2020. Everyone was asked to wash their hands before entering the main worship area and the congregation were not allowed to receive the wine from the chalice, with me receiving it on their behalf. A few days later, the whole country went into a national lockdown, meaning that all regular services held in church buildings were to be suspended.

Initially, nobody knew the extent to which this virus would go on to affect our lives. There was a lot of speculation in the media, and the government was trying its best to hurriedly bring in new laws and rules by which everyone was expected to abide, in order to stay safe and healthy. People were glued to their televisions, anxiously awaiting the daily updates. The Queen even gave a special address to the nation in an attempt to help bring a sense of calm and hope. There was great fear among the population around catching the virus. People began to panic buy at the shops, and the government gave instructions that we should only purchase what we needed for the coming week, as stocks on the shelves were running very low. Honestly, I did not feel the need to stockpile, but rather trusted God that we would have enough of what we needed to keep going. Our only concern was that the powdered formula milk our grandson needed was in short supply, and often we had to search many different stores before finding it in stock.

Personally, I did not leave the house for the first few weeks, instead taking the opportunity to unwind and relax, as I could no longer continue with my regular church duties. Leon also kept me busy during this unpredictable and scary time. I turned to prayer and tried to listen for the voice of God, in order to have peace of mind concerning this virus and what its outcome would be. What was happening to the world, and would we ever come out of this? What was God's purpose in all that was happening? There were people on social media quoting Bible verses from the book of Revelation, claiming that current events were the fulfilment of prophecy, but were they right?

Each morning Stanley and I said morning prayers together. We do this when we wake up, before getting on with the day. One particular morning, after praying, I stayed in bed with my eyes closed while Stanley got up and continued with his daily routine. After a few moments, I began to see a vision of a dark cloud in the sky going round and round as if it was chasing its tail. This went on for a long while. I waited and waited without opening my eyes as I was anxious to see the end result. And then, very slowly and gradually, the cloud began to get smaller and smaller in size until it eventually disappeared and the sky with its usual clouds began to appear. I realised that this might be a picture of the future of the virus.

I received great peace, believing it meant that though the virus was here and causing problems now, it would pass and we would get back to normal life eventually. This peace stayed with me throughout the months of strict lockdown.

A few days after getting the go-ahead to retire from the Revs Steve and Ali Taylor, I emailed the bishop's office to inform them. The bishop was fine with my decision, thanking me for my services and setting the retirement date.

That's how I slid into my official retirement. As per the bishop's previous directives, I was given the option of applying for a PTO. I decided to do this and so received my licence to enable me to carry on serving in any Anglican church, when needed, for another three years.

All the churches in the UK were swamped with many instructions and ideas on how to continue with some form of public worship during these difficult times. The best way seemed to be by making use of the latest technology (Zoom, YouTube, Facebook, etc). Owing to the concerns over keeping everyone safe and healthy, all churches, restaurants, non-essential shops and schools were closed. Only one member of each family was allowed to go into the supermarket. The wearing of face masks and the regular use of hand sanitiser was strongly encouraged. The daily death rate was on the rise and the number of free intensive care beds was becoming dangerously low. Extra temporary hospitals were hurriedly put into place to cope with the surge in demand. There also seemed to be an alarming shortage of basic protective equipment for NHS staff, such as disposable gowns and appropriate face masks. It was a very sad time for the families of the world who were losing their loved ones, especially when they died alone, with even close family being prevented from entering hospital wards.

There were, however, some positives to come out of this crisis. For example, there was a greater appreciation of those working on the frontline in the NHS, with a weekly initiative held every Thursday evening at 8pm, when everyone was encouraged to go to their front doors and clap and cheer together in appreciation for all their sacrificial work on our behalf.

At St James', when Mothering Sunday 2020 approached, all the ladies of the church were surprised to receive a pot plant left on their doorstep by other church members. Also during Holy Week we were given a prayer/meditation pack containing activities and crafts to complete each day. Every church community took various steps to keep their members' spirits high. We all prayed that some good would come out of this pandemic for the life of the Church. It was encouraging to know that even with church buildings closed, online viewing of church services had increased dramatically.

During this time of lockdown, driving test centres were closed, which meant that Stanley had no pupils to instruct. He therefore had plenty of time to spend at home with Leon and in the garden. This was a great help, allowing me to leave Stanley to do all the harder manual work! All I did was to sow some leftover seeds from the previous year, and then waited to enjoy the harvest. Rocky was working three days a week while his wife was on maternity leave at that time, after giving birth to baby Leon. In a way, it was a good time to be together and to enjoy each other's company. Rocky caught up with many DIY jobs around the house! Stanley is also quite handy and used the time to complete previously half-done jobs, not wanting to throw anything away until he had first had a go at repairing it himself.

During lockdown, various topics for sermons began coming to my mind and I thought about beginning to prepare something in case I got an opportunity to preach somewhere during my 'retirement'. Then the vicar phoned me to clarify my position now with St James', and suggested that I could preach one last official retiring sermon. I agreed and took this opportunity, nervously pre-recording my first-ever sermon via video, with it being broadcast to all four congregations via Zoom! It was my first experience of preaching to the camera on my iPad, rather than to a live, present congregation.

On the day of the broadcast, just as my sermon finished, the front doorbell rang. Over the internet the vicar, Rev Ali, said, 'Amelia, your doorbell is ringing! Aren't you going to open the door?'

I replied, 'Someone else will open it.'

Then Stanley appeared behind me saying, 'It's for you!'

I could not believe my eyes; the other vicar, Rev Steve, who had been leading the music in the service, was standing there, a few metres away, with his mask on. On the steps in front of him were two pots of flowers, gifts from St James Church, thanking me for my years of service. I was very grateful for this kind gesture, especially when he drove back to the vicarage, a good twenty minutes' journey, just to be there in time to play the piano for the final song of the church service!

This seemed a strange way to end my regular working career, but I believe that I have not finished yet. As a matter of fact, it seems like this might simply be the beginning of a new chapter. Maybe there will be future ministry opportunities ahead. I can only speculate right now, and wait for God's guidance. Looking back now, it seems like I have been in the ministry for a long time, but with God's grace and Stanley's help and provision I believe that I have been able to fulfil God's call upon my life. I like to think that I have obeyed God and accomplished what He had in mind when He first brought me to Britain.

Stanley has always been a person who plans with the long-term in mind. By God's grace, he had planned ahead for our finances for retirement, so that we should be able to live relatively comfortably. When I arrived in the UK, we only wished for a roof over our heads, but God, from His riches, has provided for all our needs. I cannot thank Him enough for His provision.

Stanley likes to be in touch with the world of politics and finance, enjoying watching the news and programmes about renovating properties. As far as his spiritual life is concerned, his faith has continued to grow quietly but steadily over the years. He took time to examine many of the world's faiths, ultimately realising that Jesus Christ holds the truth. Sometimes it feels as if he has a stronger faith than me. He is a clean-hearted person with a generous disposition, always ready and willing to help people in need. He has clear views about God and his own salvation. He says, 'I would rather have faith in a living God than a dead one!' I think of Stanley as similar to one of those individuals in the Bible who, though we read about them, are not often spoken of; they may not be considered 'superstars', yet they fulfilled God's purpose and plans in both their own lives and the lives of others.

It looks as if somehow I have come full circle, in that I am back where I began, working at home as a housewife and helping to raise our children (though now it is our grandchildren!), and preparing sermons. Along my journey of faith, I have felt enriched by the light of Christ and have been nurtured through the study of His Word (although I know I still have a lot to learn!).

Stanley and I started with just the two of us and now it's eight of us; and I can't forget the six godchildren we have gained over the years! Two are married already and the rest are in education. Praise the Lord! My desire now is to pass on this knowledge and love of Christ to my grandchildren and the generations to come – handing over the rest of my life to the divine Gardener, for whatever He wants to do.

Epilogue

Looking back, I can see God's grace at work throughout my life. My calling was not because there was anything special about me particularly. I had no outstanding ability or great knowledge, but God took me on His journey, leading me and teaching me little by little as I went along. My time working with children was a great training time, as though I was the one learning. While ministering in church there were many occasions when I felt out of my depth. I remember once, when a new priest, leading a Communion service where I missed out a whole section of the required liturgy, yet St James' congregation were very patient with me and never complained. I am very grateful for their support and understanding over the years.

For all these provisions I give the glory to God, who has sustained me and been with me throughout. Actually, He has always been at work in one way or another. As I understand it, life is a bit like a jigsaw puzzle; we can only see the whole picture when it's complete.

I would like to conclude this book by sharing some thoughts from the Bible which I have tried to live by:

- Love one another, as Jesus has loved you (John 13:34).

- Forgive, as you have been forgiven (Matthew 18:21-35; Ephesians 4:32).

- Don't take revenge, but rather leave it to God (Romans 12:19).

- Do to others as you would expect them to do to you (Luke 6:31).

- Repent, for the kingdom of God is near (Matthew 3:2; 4:17).

- Judge not and you will not be judged (Luke 6:37).

- Give, and it shall be given to you (Luke 6:38).

- Do not worry, but rather leave all your worries to God (Matthew 6:25-34; Philippians 4:6-7).

- Rejoice in God and He will give you the desires of your heart (Psalm 37:4).

- Build a deep relationship with God (Ephesians 1:15-17).

- Deal with your anger before you go to sleep (Ephesians 4:26).

- Do everything 'as working for the Lord' (Colossians 3:23).

- Be in the world, but not of the world (John 17:14-18).

- Set your mind on the things to come (Colossians 3:1-4).

Lastly, some verses from Paul's epistle to the Philippians, which I feel reflect my life, and the life of every Christian, for that matter:

> Not that I have already obtained all this, or have already arrived at my goal, but I press on to take

hold of that for which Christ Jesus took hold of me. Brothers and sisters, I do not consider myself yet to have taken hold of it. But one thing I do: forgetting what is behind and straining towards what is ahead, I press on towards the goal to win the prize for which God has called me heavenwards in Christ Jesus.
(Philippians 3:12-14)

Amen.

Final Thoughts

My thought in adding this final section to the book was to encourage women, especially those from other countries who will come to the UK after me. I have happily served within the Diocese of Willesden. It has not been without its struggles!

In the mid-eighties the idea of immigrant women in the ministry, especially women from my Pakistani background, seemed completely out of the question. I will be forever grateful to those who sensed my calling to serve God in this way.

Ever since my arrival in the UK, I have been conscious of my accent when speaking English. It felt important for me to get to the bottom of why indeed my spoken English accent had not become more English-sounding! There may well be various opinions on this subject, but here are my own. I may be totally wrong here. Speaking the Punjabi language as my mother tongue and Urdu as my official language, my certain tones and dialect make me sound like I have a strong-sounding alphabet compared to English. That's where my accent comes from and it is therefore probably never going to change. I have noticed that immigrants from other countries also make different sounds when speaking English, according to the way they have learned to speak their own mother tongue.

It also came to my attention that children who have been educated at local schools have accents much closer to those of British-born people. I noticed that those who emigrate to places such as America or Canada, or even just move to Wales or to the north of England, naturally pick up some of the local accent.

I was never questioned about my accent while serving at St James Church, despite having preached there for many years. I think the reason for this is that the church is situated in the midst of a multiracial area and they see and hear people from all sorts of backgrounds every day. By contrast, people living and working in predominantly native English-speaking areas have no such regular experiences. At St James', continuous efforts have been made to reach out to the local community with the good news of Jesus Christ, often working together with other churches in the area. For this work to prosper, it is important to show understanding and love towards people of all cultures and backgrounds.

Jesus Himself is to be our example in this matter. He took compassion on all who came to Him, regardless of their background or race. The parable of the good Samaritan is a helpful story that He once told to show us how to behave towards strangers and foreigners. Here, a Samaritan (a non-Jew) helped a man when he was attacked by robbers and left for dead at the side of the road. A passing priest and a Levite did not stop to help him. After telling this parable, Jesus asked his listeners, 'Which of these three do you think was a neighbour to the man?' An expert in the law replied, 'The one who had mercy on him.' Jesus then said, 'Go and do likewise' (Luke 10:25-37).

During his time at St James', the previous vicar, Rev John Root, made an effort to visit both India (Gujarat) and Pakistan (Karachi, Peshawar, Islamabad and Lahore), in order to learn more about their culture and church life. While there, he met up with local missionaries, clergy and bishops, and was invited to preach at the cathedrals in both Lahore and Peshawar. He also visited the seminary in Gujranwala. I caught up with him in Rawalpindi, near Islamabad, when he happened to be visiting my brother and his family, and we were able to worship together at an international church there.

My calling to become a priest was seen as controversial back in 1994, especially among more traditional conservative Christians, but I felt convinced that this was the path that God was leading me down. In Jesus' time, the Jewish culture was one where women were not allowed to lead or teach men, just like in many countries today; women had to find other ways of serving in the church. I, however, saw that equality between men and women is taught within the Scriptures:

> There is neither Jew nor Gentile, neither slave nor free, nor is there male and female, for you are all one in Christ Jesus. If you belong to Christ, then you are Abraham's seed, and heirs according to the promise.
> (Galatians 3:28-29)

This was one of the main Bible verses giving me assurance that my calling was in line with God's will, along with the accounts of the lives of the many faithful women in the Bible who served God in many different ways.

God's call is not always an easy one; it can contain much training and preparation in order to mould someone until they are ready to fulfil His purposes. Moses is a prime example of this. We find his story in the book of Exodus. As a baby, he was put into a papyrus basket and placed in the Nile to protect him from being killed. Pharaoh's daughter saw him and took him from the water, bringing him up in the palace as her own son. He murdered an Egyptian when he saw him beating one of his fellow Hebrews. Moses then fled to Midian, in fear for his life, and there he came to the aid of some young women, protecting them from nearby shepherds and helping them to draw water for their flocks. They were all daughters of a local priest, and one of them, Zipporah, was given to him in marriage. Moses said about himself, 'I have become a foreigner in a foreign land' (Exodus 2:22), naming his firstborn son 'Gershom', meaning 'a foreigner there'.

He served his father-in-law for forty years as a shepherd before encountering God in the burning bush and returning to Egypt to rescue the Israelites from their bondage. I believe that Moses was chosen from birth by God for this purpose, but he needed to be both trained and humbled by God before he was ready to be the leader God wanted him to be.

Mary Magdalene was a woman who had 'seven demons' cast out of her (Luke 8:2). She was one of the earliest followers of Jesus. According to the Bible, she travelled with Jesus, witnessed His crucifixion and was one of the first people to meet Jesus after His resurrection.

I take courage from the fact that God can take an outcast woman, transform her life and use her for His purposes.

We read in 1 Samuel 16 the story of how the prophet Samuel was sent by God to choose the new king to replace King Saul when he turned away from God. Samuel was sent to Bethlehem to anoint one of Jesse's sons. After seeing Eliab, he assumed that he must be the one, but God said to him, 'The LORD does not look at the things people look at. People look at the outward appearance, but the LORD looks at the heart' (1 Samuel 16:7). In the end, the youngest of all, David, the shepherd boy, was chosen by God and anointed by Samuel to be the future king. God is the one who chooses and His criteria are not the same as the world's!

When I arrived in the UK I had no great assumptions about my future life in London, but I always had peace that God was with me and that He would guide me in the future as well. While observing the Christian Pakistani community around us, I learned a great deal. They were the first immigrants I met here and I saw myself as one of them. I took the opportunity to learn from both their positive and their negative experiences of settling into a new country, and tried my best to choose what was right for my family. Our children became friends with their children and learned from them too.

My experience at Oak Hill Theological College was predominantly a welcoming and accepting one. Although I was the only Asian in my year group, I was never questioned about my background, ethnicity or accent, even though I always wore my regular Pakistani-style clothing. It is probable that they understood the multicultural history of the Church and knew something of God's heart for all people.

When I took up my role at St James', in the Diocese of Willesden, I did not always find my place within the diocese straightforward. I was a part-time, non-stipendiary minister, who also had a part-time job five afternoons a week. I often chose only to attend the clergy chapter meetings that were close by so that I could get back in time for my afternoon job. Back then there were few additional meetings specifically for NSM clergy, though nowadays there seems to be more support provided. I knew only a few of the full-time clergy, only those who held key roles or who had previously been curates at St James'. Many of the clergy seemed to meet up regularly and had lots to talk about together, such as how things were going in their parish and various issues and aspects of church ministry. I did feel a little bit on the periphery of things when we met up.

Something else that I came to realise was that, as an Asian woman, I was still culturally expected to do the majority of the household duties at home – cooking, cleaning, washing and taking care of the children – fulfilling my church and work duties on top of this. Times are changing now, though, and maybe this would not be so much the case for second-generation British Pakistani women.

As a mother and now a mother-in-law I also feel that I have quite an important role in the sense of being a good example, treating everyone equally and with respect, and promoting unity within the family. Differences of opinion can sometimes arise between different family members, and I see that my role is to be that of a family peacekeeper!

All cultures have different family traditions that they follow. Some Pakistani immigrants still hold on to the tradition of having the extended family all living together under one roof. On the other hand, the new generation is turning away more and more from this tradition, often preferring to live more independently.

I personally did not have the experience of living with my mother-in-law and so never knew how I would have been treated in such a situation. Would I have been treated like a daughter, or as someone less than that? It certainly is good to remember that, as a new wife, there was so much that I did not know back then, and had to learn as I went along, and so I should now not be quick to judge, but rather be humble and understanding. This new relationship is not always easy to keep and maintain in a close-knit family. These kinds of thoughts were brewing in the back of my mind when my children began growing up, long before they got married.

When differences of opinion arise, I need to remember my role as a Christian mother, showing the love of God, allowing it to flow from my own life and attitudes. We can also overlook the generation gap that now exists, so expectations that once existed when we were young may well have changed now.

I want to treat my daughter-in-law as I would my own daughter. Similarly, I would want my daughter to be treated this way by her mother-in-law. I hope to show this more by the example of my actions rather than by just my words. They are, after all, going to be the future mothers and mothers-in-law of the next generation.

Scripture reminds us that we like to give the best to our children – see, for example, Matthew 7:11. Similarly, we can try to do this for our grandchildren, if we have them, to enrich them with the love of God shown in Jesus Christ, who is the provider of all good gifts. They may well have more understanding of technology and the modern world that surrounds us, but we, as the more experienced ones, are those who should take up the task of showing them the right path to take in this busy, fast-paced life. We need to learn to be content in life, and to my mind, this seems to have been fading away recently. With the fast development of technology, the temptation is to be always trying to stay up to date with it all. This is common among the younger generation but the older generation are slower paced and as a result may well be more content with what we already have. This is one reason that the generation gap between us has grown even bigger in our families – English and Asian alike.

One needs to learn that respect and understanding between the generations is important. The older generation have a greater experience of life in general, whereas the younger generation may well have a better grasp of modern-day life. Paul addresses this theme in his letter to the church in Ephesus:

> Children, obey your parents in the Lord, for this is right. 'Honour your father and mother' – which is the first commandment with a promise – 'so that it may go well with you and that you may enjoy long life on the earth.'
> Fathers, do not exasperate your children; instead, bring them up in the training and instruction of the Lord.
> (Ephesians 6:1-4)

Being both a Christian and an immigrant settled in another country, I believe that God was with me and that he had His purposes to fulfil. I had a sense of hope that all would be well. When God told Abraham to leave his country, his people and his father's household and travel to a distant land, God promised him that He would make his descendants into 'a great nation'. His name would be 'great' and those who blessed him would be blessed and those who cursed him would be cursed. He would be a blessing to the whole earth (Genesis 12:1-3)!

I am thinking here of everyone whom God takes to other parts of the world to live. We leave everything behind but we still take our culture with us. We find ourselves split between two countries and two cultures; our hearts are always partly with our homeland. Perhaps it is good to realise here that no country is our true home, but rather our true home is to be with Christ in the New Creation!

Although we enrich the country we settle in with our talents and gifts, we have many new things to learn. There has to be give and take for good integration with the local community. This process can bring us into a deeper understanding of both our neighbours and ourselves, and can help us to grow in love and tolerance towards other cultures and faiths – we are sent out as the light of Christ. Our primary purpose is to spread the good news of Jesus Christ into the dark corners of the world. The whole world is open to us with such opportunities. Even countries considered 'closed' to Christian mission are often open to receive those coming to work there who are skilled in a specific profession. After we learn the language and the culture of the land that we find ourselves in, then the doors are often opened wide to us, both for our growth and to be able to share about Christ.

The first generation of Christian Pakistanis who came to the UK found it hard in many ways to integrate. Problems in speaking fluent English were quite a barrier initially. As a result, they found it difficult to worship freely in their local churches, and so tended to form their own Urdu-language fellowships. These fellowship groups can, however, have quite a short life, as the second generation often don't read or write in the mother tongue of their parents. As a result, this second generation can end up not going to church at all, and lose the opportunity to both learn the Scriptures and form lasting Christian friendships. It has been a hard lesson to learn, but good can still come if Christian migrant parents are prepared to get involved in their local churches and take their children along with them, so that they might be fully part of church life there. I am just trying to make a general observation here that I hope can help future generations to grow and mature in Christ.

Personally, I feel that it is important for Christians newly arriving in a country to join a local branch of their regular church denomination, where possible. Having said that, one does need to listen to the voice of the Lord, and find a church where His truth is preached, and where one can grow and contribute to the life of the church. No church is perfect, because 'the Church' is the people, not the building or the denomination, and people are never perfect! However, we can pray about any shortfalls and weaknesses that we find there, being careful not to judge, rather leaving all judgement to God. As long as the Lord

Himself is guiding the church, we can take heart that *He* is the head, and is in full sovereign control.

My generation of women can sometimes be particularly reluctant to explore life beyond their own culture and race, perhaps because they have often been expected to stay at home while their husbands went out to work. May I take this opportunity to encourage other women from different cultures to take heart and trust the God who has brought us to this part of the world to fully explore life in the UK? We have opportunities and freedoms here to raise our voices against the injustices and inequalities experienced by many women and children in the developing world. Issues such as racism, hatred against different faiths and even slavery are still very real areas of concern in our world today, and we can all play our part in standing up against such evils. Prayer is a powerful weapon to be used by godly men and women in combating these injustices. The person of Jesus Christ can prevail in the hearts of the hard-hearted to make our world a place more ready for His kingdom to come.

Since my arrival in the UK, I have been in a continuous learning mode, concerning all areas of my life. I had an expectation of learning from everyone I came in contact with. Having a quiet nature myself, I tend to be an attentive listener and then think over what has been said. As a result, I take things to heart, which can be both positive and negative. I saw how I was accepted (or not!) by the world around me and tried to adjust accordingly, in order to fit in. I trusted God that good would come out of it for me eventually, and indeed it did. I learned tolerance, perseverance and how sometimes it is best to simply leave things with God for Him to resolve.

Recently there has been a fresh voice against racism heard throughout the world, coming after George Floyd's death in the USA, where an unarmed black man suffocated while being arrested by police. I thought that our children, the new generation, would have no such issues like this in their lives, but this has sadly proved not to be the case.

On a different note, there are some other things that, as an Asian woman, I noticed. British people tend to say 'please', 'thank you' and 'sorry' much more than we do, and it can take decades to adjust! A common thing that comes to mind is what happens when phoning Asian friends. I often hear, 'You have not called me in a while.' For me this gets a bit uncomfortable to keep hearing over and over again! I tend to just listen and carry on with the conversation, saying, 'I have been busy,' or something similar. There are many more things like this that can occur, which can hinder good relationships within our community. Timekeeping is another area in which we as an Asian community have a lot to learn!

I need to be careful about what I say to others, as I can sometimes speak without thinking of the consequences. This is something that we as a Christian community can be particularly guilty of. We are told in Scripture to '[speak] the truth in love' (Ephesians 4:15), not simply to just speak out whatever we perceive to be correct at the time. By adhering to this verse, we won't hurt others unnecessarily, but rather keep communication channels open and help maintain good relationships. This passage goes on to say:

> Do not let any unwholesome talk come out of
> your mouths, but only what is helpful for
> building others up according to their needs, that
> it may benefit those who listen. And do not grieve
> the Holy Spirit.
> (Ephesians 4:29-30)

Another thing I have learned in my life is how to react when grudges and perceived hurts go round and round in our minds. God's Word tells us to 'rid yourselves of all malice' (1 Peter 2:1). Such thoughts are obviously put into our minds by the evil one, Satan, who comes to tear apart families and communities. For these kinds of issues, we need to pray to God. Confessing such things with a prayer partner can be useful here – I myself have found this helpful.

The point I am making is that we are to keep our heart clean towards others as much as we can. After all, we are answerable to God, who dwells in us! Jesus tells us, 'Do not judge, or you too will be judged. For in the same way as you judge others, you will be judged, and with the measure you use, it will be measured to you' (Matthew 7:1-2). We need to live in the light of Christ by renewing our thoughts and attitudes. Paul writes, 'Get rid of all bitterness, rage and anger, brawling and slander, along with every form of malice. Be kind and compassionate to one another, forgiving each other, just as in Christ God forgave you' (Ephesians 4:31-32). Lastly, Jesus told His disciples, 'Whoever wants to be my disciple must deny themselves and take up their cross and follow me' (Matthew 16:24).

Many of us feel the need to offload our family frustrations to someone. A common habit we might have is to share our burdens with anyone we meet. This may backfire on us and we can end up more depressed when confidences are betrayed. It is better to pray and ask God about finding a trustworthy friend who will be able to listen without being judgemental; someone wise enough to keep our discussions to themselves, to pray with us and to wait for God's answers. Such a person is a very precious friend to have.

One thing I have felt very helpful personally is to go away on my own periodically, for a short spiritual retreat. I have often stayed at a local convent, just for three or four days. I have my own room, access to the chapel and meals provided, if I so desire. I use the time to be quiet, to read the Scriptures, to pray and to listen for God's voice. It can also be a great time of rest, to switch off from the regular stresses of life. I always come back feeling refreshed and closer to God.

As I look back, I see that God never revealed all my future steps to me all at once, but rather showed me just enough for what I should do next, and then called me to trust Him for what lay beyond that. I think of the biblical stories of Abraham and Moses, who were called to follow God and step out in faith, without fully knowing where they were going, or how their lives and future ministry would evolve.

Even at the end of our lives here on earth we might not fully understand our life's path, but as Paul writes in 1 Corinthians 13:12: 'For now we see only a reflection as in a mirror; then we shall see face to face. Now I know in part; then I shall know fully, even as I am fully known.'

Acknowledgements

I would like to thank everyone who helped make this book possible. Especially St James Church members, clergy (past and present), my entire family, friends and colleagues – without their ongoing support, this would not have been an easy task.

I am grateful to Sanila Gill and to the late Rev Bryan Wadland for reading the very first draft for me.

For David Shaw's dedicated and committed service right through the book, even working online to make suggestions and to help get the sentences in the correct order. His help has been invaluable.

I am grateful to all the endorsers for their time to read and to make encouraging comments.

To all the team at Instant Apostle for agreeing to publish my story and for working hard on it to make it what it is.